The Mediaeval Academy of America
Publication No. 83

Boethian Fictions

Boethian Fictions

Narratives in the Medieval French
Versions of the Consolatio Philosophiae

RICHARD A. DWYER
Florida International University

The Mediaeval Academy of America
Cambridge, Massachusetts   1976

The publication of this book was made possible by grants of funds to the Mediaeval Academy from the Carnegie Corporation of New York.

In memory of
William Matthews

Contents

Illustrations

Preface

THIS STUDY of the literary significance of narratives in the medieval French translations of Boethius's *Consolatio philosophiae* began in the library stacks of the University of California at Los Angeles and has occupied me intermittently during my tenure at Purdue University, the University of Florida and at Florida International University. But the bulk of research was done in the summer of 1969 at the Bibliothèque Nationale, the British Museum, and the Bodleian Library, to whose officers and staffs I am deeply grateful for giving me access to manuscripts and permission to quote from them. For help with the transcriptions I must thank Margaret W. Epro and William Roach of the University of Pennsylvania. Portions of this study have appeared in one form or another in *Romance Philology, Annuale Mediaevale, The Chaucer Review* and elsewhere. Financially, the project has been supported by grants from the academic Councils of the University of Florida and from the American Philosophical Society. In the ultimate stages of its writing, this study has profited from the close reading given it by friends and colleagues, especially the late William Matthews, to whom I dedicate this work, and Lynn White, Jr., of the University of California, Los Angeles, John Algeo of the University of Georgia, and Luke Wenger of the Mediaeval Academy of America. Because I have not accepted all of their suggestions, I must take more than the customary responsibility for the remaining infelicities. To many other persons—my wife Roxanne, friends, colleagues, librarians, and typists—I owe a large, and by now uncollectable, debt.

Introduction

AN UNLIKELY EMBLEM comes to mind concerning the medieval Boethius. In one of the upper rooms of smaller Egyptian antiquities in the Louvre is a statuette of the hawk-headed god Horus clad in the ceremonial armor of a Roman centurion, his fierce little head craning out of the hammered breastplate. The effect is startling and serves as a reminder of how ancient are the processes of cultural assimilation and how curious their products can be. Although more than a millenium farther along in time, the late medieval French versions of the *Consolatio philosophiae* are another such set of products, and to them and to the processes of making Boethius medieval that bronze figure relates as well. For one thing, the same Alexandria that saw the meeting of Antony and Cleopatra also witnessed the encounter between Christian revelation and Neoplatonic speculation, the two poles of an intellectual tension in Boethius that exercised scholars—and translators—throughout the Middle Ages. But it is in the prospect of giving new dress to old icons that the statuette makes its most pointed lesson, for we shall see in the course of this study how continuously the medieval translators were diverted from the pursuit of the naked truth by their fascination with Philosophy's garments—her *integument* as they called it. And in the end they themselves succeeded in outfitting her in modes that Boethius would surely have found strange but, perhaps, comely.

Some of the medieval reverberation of Boethius was picked up by the surveys of Howard R. Patch on the traditions of Boethius and the goddess Fortuna.[1] His notices of the enthusiastic reception of the *Consolatio philosophiae* and its many indirect influences in the Middle Ages have since been supplemented by the more detailed work of French scholars both on medieval Latin commentary on the text and on its vernacular translators. Recently Pierre Courcelle probed the cultural significance of the shifting Latin commentary and the reflexes of the *Consolatio* in

---

1. Howard R. Patch, *The Goddess Fortuna in Mediaeval Literature* (Cambridge, Mass., 1927); *The Tradition of Boethius* (New York, 1935).

iconography and Latin literature.[2] And not very long ago such students as Antoine Thomas, Mario Roques, and V. L. Dedeck-Héry extensively examined the linguistic and bibliographic aspects of some of the French translations.[3] No one, however, has looked at all thirteen of them from a literary point of view to determine whether they actually transmute the *Consolatio* into a medieval work and show any art in doing so.

In this study I have undertaken a portion of this task. I concentrate on those half-dozen versions of the *Consolatio* that freely diverge from the Boethian text and specifically on the parts of those versions showing significant narrative interpolations. The discussion of these narratives is conducted under three heads: fable, history, and integument, terms customarily linked to the ways medieval commentators read the Bible. Here they simply indicate three different kinds of stories: pure fiction versus historically-based narratives, and tales that are allegorically interpreted. The fate of allegory in these vernacular versions is significant. The interpolations of the later translators become characterized by such a compelling interest in narrative that the allusive mode of the Boethian original is altered, and the allegorical interpretations of the Latin schoolmen fall by the wayside. The most successful narratives I see as both "medievalizing" and "universalizing" aspects of Boethius in something of the senses in which C. S. Lewis used these words to name the ways Chaucer transmuted Boccaccio's *Il Filostrato* into the *Troilus*.[4] Just as it

2. Pierre Courcelle, *La Consolation de philosophie dans la tradition littéraire* (Paris, 1967).

3. Antoine Thomas and Mario Roques, "Traductions françaises de la *Consolatio Philosophiae* de Boèce," in *Histoire littéraire de la France* 37 (Paris, 1938):419–88; V. L. Dedeck–Héry, "The Manuscripts of the Translation of Boethius' *Consolatio* by Jean de Meung," *Speculum* 15 (1940):432–443. Earlier surveys of the versions include: Leopold Delisle, "Anciennes traductions françaises de la Consolation de Boèce conservée à la Bibliothèque Nationale," *Bibliothèque de l'École des Chartes* 34 (1873):5–32; G. Gröber, *Grundriss der romanischen Philologie* 2, 1 (Strassburg, 1902): 746–7; Charles-Victor Langlois, "La 'consolation' de Boèce d'après Jean de Meun et plusieurs autres," in *La Vie en France au Moyen âge*, 4 vols. (Paris, 1928), 4:269–326. More recent bibliographic work: Louise W. Stone, "Old French Trans. of the *De Cons. Phil.* of Boethius: Some Unnoticed MSS," *Medium Aevum* 6 (1937):21–30; A. Van der Vyver, "Les Traductions du *De Cons. Phil.* en littérature comparée," *Humanisme et Renaissance* 6 (1939): 247–73; and the present author's "Manuscripts of the Medieval French Boethius," *Notes & Queries* (1971):124–5.

4. C. S. Lewis, "What Chaucer Really Did to *Il Filostrato*," *Essays and Studies* 17 (1932):56–75.

is more typically medieval and universal, claims Lewis, to make Herod your villain than it is to make Tamburlaine your hero, so is it to sing of Death the Leveler and Asinus the Astonomer in place of the praises of stoic fortitude and Neoplatonic *nous.*

Few things make the neglect of these translations intelligible, for even a glance at Thomas's articles reveals hints of rich narrative dilations in many of the translations. But the situation today is still largely what it was in 1936 when E. T. Silk remarked that for some time to come students of Boethius's influence would have to concern themselves with unpublished materials. Since his remark only one of these thirteen translations has been edited—that of Jean de Meun—and for the study of interpolated narrative that version is one of the least interesting.[5]

Some of the reasons for this neglect are linguistic and bibliographical. Of the early prose versions, the four that are extant in unique MSS are also in unusual dialects, while two of the verse versions exist in over thirty MSS each, and one mixed version has survived in about fifty copies. There are other obstacles to editing, reminiscent of those Pierre Courcelle encountered in attempting to identify and classify MSS of the commentaries: "Ces commentaires se plagient les uns les autres, et telle glose du IXe siècle peut se retrouver intégralement dans un commentaire du XVe."[6] It is clear, for example, that some sort of borrowing relationship exists among seven of the thirteen translations considered here; and because it is clear, I am sure that many a prospective editor has shied from the task. I have sought a compromise. Because many of the texts I discuss are either unpublished or available only in fragments or obscure printings, I have included in an appendix a very generous sample of the narratives to be found in these translations. But I have indicated variant readings only where I could see some literary reason for their existence. Without apologizing for the obvious limitations of this procedure, let me say that I have been very solicitous of interesting variants and have rejected a great many of the other kind. Finally, I must add that I am no Romance philologist and would wish that I had been preceded by a few technical experts into parts of this remote, but rich country. Because the vernacular versions have a clear though limited relation to the tradition of Latin

5. V. L. Dedeck–Héry, "Boethius' *De Consolatione* by Jean de Meun," *Mediaeval Studies* 14 (1952):165–275. Other editions are in progress.
6. Courcelle, p. 13.

commentary, I will briefly survey the course of scholastic interest in the *Consolatio* before turning to the translations.

The *Consolatio philosophiae* was composed around 524—in the prison of Pavia according to legend—and became one of the works of late classical antiquity that medieval authors knew best and cited most willingly. For seven centuries it remained a classic to be commented on in the schools and continuously recopied. Between the Carolingian period and the end of the fifteenth century almost three dozen commentaries were written on the work. This continuous intellectual interest seems to have been guaranteed by Boethius's dual and ambiguous role as philosophical authority and Christian martyr. The following sketch of that interest draws most heavily on the account by Pierre Courcelle.[7]

It is difficult for us to comprehend the doctrinal agonies that the *Consolatio* provoked in its medieval students. We are usually introduced to it as a mild dialogue of self-comfort by Gibbon's remark that "it is a golden volume worthy of the leisure of Plato or Tully." But would a volume fit for that audience prove equally diverting to Innocent III or St. Bernard? The *Consolatio philosophiae,* in truth, seems to be a kind of apocalypse in which the envisioned personification of purely Human Wisdom restores the narrator's mental health by a guided course of Neo-platonic metaphysics, a course raised to almost sacramental dignity by the resources of late Latin rhetoric and poetics. Many medieval readers caught in it a glimpse, otherwise denied, of the strange doctrines of the last pagan school of Alexandria and its predecessors: Porphyry, Proclus, Ammonius, Olympiodorus and others. For the commentators, these doctrines—reminiscence, the pre-existence and "chariot" of the soul, the world soul and the perpetuity of the world, and the intermediaries of Providence and Fortune—proved to be, from the very beginning, obstacles to accepting Boethius as a Christian authority.

That beginning, nevertheless, was impressive. Rediscovered and promoted by Alcuin, the *Consolatio* enjoyed a considerable vogue among Carolingian commentators, and the earliest known commentary is apparently one of the best. It is preserved, among other places, in two anonymous manuscripts of St. Gall, where it may have been composed around 870 and used by Notker a century later for his Old High German version of Boethius. Up to the crucial meter 9 of Book III, the author attempts a

---

7. Courcelle, pp. 241–344.

straightforward Christian interpretation of Boethius at the cost, according to Courcelle, of several subtle distortions. Thus, Philosophy is both the Wisdom of God and Christ Himself on different occasions. When confronted, finally, with the Neoplatonic theories mentioned above, the monk falters, as many have since, and acknowledges that not all that Boethius wrote may conform to dogma. Vatican MS Lat. 3363 contains certain interlinear glosses which may represent a revision of the St. Gall version, possibly made by the English Bishop Asser, for some such commentary seems to lie behind the Christianizing interpolations to be found in King Alfred's translation of the *Consolatio*. Among other early Carolingian commentaries may be counted that of Lupus of Ferrières (d. 862) on the verses, and a conjectured one by John Scotus Eriugena (d. 877), posited as a source of his ideas in the most influential early commentary, that of Remigius of Auxerre, nephew of Lupus.

Around 902 Remigius compiled a commentary that survives in one form or another in about thirty manuscripts. In the course of identifying the Second Vatican Mythographer as Remigius, Courcelle describes his typical method: he commented on Boethius with the aid of the First Mythographer, the *Narrationes fabularum* of Lactantius Placidus and the commentary on Statius attributed to the same Lactantius. But at the same time, Remigius interpolated into this commentary on Statius the gloss which he had composed on Boethius. Finally, with the aid of the First Mythographer, the two works of Lactantius Placidus, and the interpolation drawn from his own commentary on Boethius, Remigius ingeniously composed his own mythography and attempted to give to it a certain unity. Courcelle speaks of him as a tireless annotator who would sacrifice nothing antique, even doctrines that tended to heresy, and who showed an indulgent ingenuity in sanitizing for his students many troublesome Boethian notions. An anonymous commentary in Brussels MS 10066–77 is no less Eriugenan than Remigius, according to Courcelle, but it is better documented and written.

Such enthusiasts were too much for Bovo of Corvey (d. 890). This vigilant abbot saw in the doctrines of the *Consolatio* and in the explications of Remigius a clear and present danger. With impartiality, he moves through the *Consolatio* pointing to what must go and what a good Christian may accept. In Courcelle's view, Bovo needed only a more direct knowledge of the actual content of Platonic doctrine to reach an objective understanding of the merits of Boethian philosophy. Directly in response to Bovo's criticism, the anonymous author of a commentary in a tenth-century Einsiedeln manuscript supplied a scholarly interpretation of the *Consolatio* based in part on Chalcidius's translation of the *Timaeus,* and the commentary of Remigius itself was sympathetically revised. Content merely to provide accurate readings of an historical document, these efforts complement Bovo's, although none of them influenced the French translations of Boethius as did the following work.

Adalbold, Bishop of Utrecht (d. 1027), wrote a commentary on Book III, meter 9, of the *Consolatio*—if there was more it has been lost—that is noteworthy for more than its thoroughly sympathetic reading of Boethius. For one thing it shows that even in the eleventh century the *Consolatio* was still being studied in the light of Remigius's interpretation. Secondly, Adalbold explicated by means of a harmony of pagan and Christian philosophers, tumbling together citations from Hermes, Plato, David, John the Evangelist, St. Jerome, and the commentaries of Boethius on Porphyry and of Gregory on St. Matthew. All of this testimony allows Adalbold to find for Plato on nearly every issue, including the world soul. Finally, the commentary is important from our point of view because it was translated in its entirety and inserted into the first French translation of the *Consolatio*—the only instance of so partial an exposition of Boethian Platonism reaching the vernacular.

After Adalbold, nothing further on the *Consolatio* appeared in the eleventh century, but the vigorous defence of Boethian Platonism begun by Remigius and continued by Adalbold reappeared and reached its apogee in the commentary of William of Conches (ca. 1125). But where the earlier commentators distorted Boethius to render him more safely Christian, the celebrated scholar of Paris and Chartres makes Platonism Christian by fiat, and those pagan myths that might, if taken literally, have proved distracting, go down easily in the honey of allegory. In the midst of long scholastic digressions on the theory of tides or mythological explications taken directly from Remigius, William defends against real opponents his distinctive beliefs. Most of these find their focus in Book III, meter 9, where, for example, Plato is found guiltless of the belief that creation took place in two steps—first a chaos of elements and then their orderly arrangement. As William sees it, the operation of natural laws on created matter is all that is needed to explain the evolution of men from mud by evaporation caused by the stars. This, of course, accords perfectly with scripture: "et hoc in divina pagina invenitur: hominem esse factum de limo terrae."

Courcelle calls attention to four anonymous commentaries from the twelfth century which reflect the influence of William's extreme views, either by paraphrasing them or strongly contesting them. None of these, however, exerted an effect on the French translations. While no new commentaries survive from the thirteenth century, St. Thomas Aquinas did appeal to Boethius in defending Aristotle from Augustine's reproach on the issue of the perpetuity of the world. This new taste for Aristotle is strong in the commentary written by the English Dominican friar, Nicholas Trevet, sometime before 1307. This most popular of medieval commentaries (Courcelle lists 42 MSS) relies heavily on the work of William of Conches—identified merely as *commentator*—and disagrees extensively with it. Everywhere the Platonism of Chartres is attacked and replaced with the Aristotelian interpretations increasingly in vogue in the thirteenth century. Trevet rejects, for example, the identification of the world soul with the Holy Spirit and goes on to reduce that force to the motions imparted to the celestial spheres by the prime mover. In Courcelle's view, Trevet is a popularizing plagiarist, although Charles Jourdain's earlier assessment was more sympathetic. In any case, Trevet's commentary was very influential on the French translations of Boethius, particularly that made by his fellow Dominican, Renaut de Louhans.

Throughout the remainder of the Middle Ages, and despite the appearance of a dozen new commentaries, the *Consolatio* in Courcelle's view ceased to exercise the vital influence it had in earlier centuries. The commentary of Tholomaeus de Asinariis mildly Christianizes Boethius and prudently defends him and Plato against the assaults of Trevet, while that of William of Aragon excuses Boethius because of his work on Aristotle. The fourteenth and fifteenth-century studies, theses, and dialogues on the *Consolatio* by Pierre d'Ailly (ca. 1372), William of Cortumelia, Denis the Carthusian, and Arnoul Greban are variously characterized by Courcelle as derivative, ponderous, systemmatic, and tendentious. Following them, the humanists Jodocus Badius Ascensius and Niccolo Perotti tended to take the *Consolatio* as a literary masterpiece fit for stylistic analysis and comparison to Horace. Of the late medieval commentaries mentioned by Courcelle, only that of Regnier of Saint Trond (ca. 1381) found its way directly into the French translations, while that of Pierre de Paris is, as we shall see, a Latin translation of his French original.

The continuous medieval scholastic interest in the *Consolatio* is thus owing to the venerable status of its Christian author, to its value as a literary work of art, and to its usefulness as a philosophical summa full

of attractions and dangers. Both of these latter were to be found in the
noble but obscure meter 9 of Book III. The world view there expounded
did not deceive most medieval commentators, but those who attempted
to render it ideologically orthodox failed by their tendentiousness, while
those who relished its exotic doctrines had acquired a taste not available
to ordinary medieval mortals. There can thus be little doubt that in the
world of Latin scholasticism the *Consolatio* was what Courcelle calls a
ferment of humanism. But by a curious turn, at the moment humanism
triumphed Boethius was laid aside. Throughout the Middle Ages he had
been a stimulus, but for those who acquired the new ability to read his
Greek sources, his work became a superannuated trot, at best a "golden
volume." The response of the vernacular culture was different and in
some ways more authentically medieval. We shall see that the vernacular
translators did make some use of the long tradition of commentary on the
Consolatio, but, unwilling or unable to assimilate its stimulating doctrines,
they turned the account of Boethius's resolute recovery into a palliative
of fables.

Before becoming available in the *langue d'oil,* the *Consolatio philosophiae* enjoyed four centuries of a vernacular circulation which by the
end of the Middle Ages extended into such languages as Catalan and
Greek. Before the end of the ninth century the text was accessible in
England, and later in Germany, in translations which both paraphrased
and annotated the original. King Alfred produced a version in Old English
prose and later versified the parts of this version representing meter in
the original in accordance with alliterative traditions.[8] Notker Labeo
(d. 1022), teacher in the school of St. Gall—or his pupils—made a version
in Old High German. The Provençal *Boëcis* might be thought to be the
earliest Romance version, but since scholars have identified it as a quasi-
hagiographical poem *about* Boethius,[9] the earliest version of the *Consolatio* in a Romance language in fact appears in the Anglo-Norman dialect
of French. This version, the *Roman de philosophie,* is a poem of 1658
lines and was composed by Simund de Freine, Canon of Hereford, around

---

8. See F. Anne Payne, *King Alfred and Boethius* (Madison, 1969), and Larry D.
   Benson, "The Literary Character of Anglo–Saxon Formulaic Poetry," *PMLA* 81
   (1966):334–41.
9. *Boëcis: poème sur Boèce,* ed. and trans. René Lavaud and Georges Machicot
   (Toulouse, 1950).

1180.[10] It freely paraphrases about a quarter of Boethius's proses and meters, suppressing all proper names and their associated narratives but adding the homely, naturalistic observations characteristic of Anglo-Norman interests.

These appearances of the Boethius in peripheral dialects are symptomatic of the linguistic problem that reduced the popularity of four of the early French versions of the *Consolatio,* and there was no widely acceptable Romance version before Jean de Meun's. The language of central France was cautiously approached as versions were made first in Anglo-Norman, then in Burgundian and Wallonian, and by such outsiders as the Sicilian Bonaventura da Demena and Pierre de Paris, who despite his name was no Parisian. A sort of linguistic stability was finally achieved in the translation by Jean de Meun, and it found instant popularity. On this prose base, the processes of manuscript transmission began to work as successive revisions and compilations refined the text linguistically and doctrinally, while revisions of a later efflorescence of verse translations refined a new host of narrative elaborations on the Boethian text.

Setting aside Simund de Freine's incomplete paraphrase, we find the earliest and one of the most interesting of the French translations of the *Consolatio* in a manuscript from the middle of the thirteenth century now preserved in the Österreichische Nationalbibliothek in Vienna, MS 2642 (Thomas I).[11] This version, made by a Burgundian about whom we know nothing beyond his intense desire to make as good a case as possible for Boethius, is continuously interrupted by short glosses drawn mostly from the twelfth-century commentary of William of Conches, with narrative supplements from the Vatican Mythographies. The longest exception to the borrowings from William is a gloss of twenty manuscript pages appended to the translation of Book III, meter 9. This gloss is a translation of all that remains of the Christianizing commentary on the *Consolatio* written by Bishop Adalbold of Utrecht (d. 1027).[12] Not only is the

10. *Les Oeuvres de Simund de Freine,* ed. John E. Matzke, Société des anciens textes français (Paris, 1909). See also M. Dominica Legge, *Anglo–Norman Literature and its Background* (Oxford, 1963), p. 184.
11. Identifications in parentheses refer first to Thomas and Roques, *HLF* and second to L. Delisle, "Anciennes traductions." For a tabular conspectus of all versions, see Appendix 2.
12. Source identified by Courcelle, "Étude critique sur les commentaires de la Consolation de Boèce (IXe–XVe siècles)," *Archives d'histoire doctrinale et littéraire du moyen âge* 14 (1939):95.

Burgundian translation doctrinally interesting, its narrative borrowings supply topics for discussion in all four chapters of this study, although its primary use here will be to establish in the first chapter the distinctions among fable, history, and integument that will govern the bulk of my discussion.

A second prose translation of the *Consolatio* survives from the end of the thirteenth century, preserved in MS 898 of the Bibliothèque of Troyes in a fine hand of the following century (Thomas II). Thomas identifies the dialect of its unknown author as Wallonian and points to his mediocre knowledge of Latin.[13] The translator made very little use of the commentaries then available, left blank the proper names unknown to him, and omitted many passages in the course of his translation; in particular, meters 4 and 5 and prose 5 of each of the last two books. Generally, it is a poor performance. No use is made of it in this investigation.

A third early prose translation into French is that made by a Sicilian, one Bonaventura da Demena (Thomas VIII, Delisle V). The region is the hinterland of Messina, and Bonaventura may have composed his version under the patronage of Charles of Anjou. It survives in a single MS that was assigned by Delisle to the fourteenth century. This MS, B. N. fr. 821, I believe to be from the latter half of the thirteenth century, making the translation possibly earlier than those of Pierre de Paris or Jean de Meun.

Bonaventura, who claims to have produced an earlier version of the *Consolatio* in "vulgar Latin," that is, Italian, wanted to give a "novelle maniere de conte a une mout utiele esscriture." The result is a work that has been called an imitation by Paulin Paris and a travesty by Thomas. It appears to have been most misunderstood by Louis Moland who printed an excerpt from it which he said attested to "l'esprit persifleur et facétieux" of the fourteenth century.[14] The question of intention implicit here need not be raised, for all the evidence tends to show Bonaventura as a pious cleric, solicitous for the instruction of his flock, and so little conscious of the translator's servile path that he repairs Lady Philosophy's neglect of Christian doctrine by inserting into his text the Ten Commandments and other counsels of perfection from the New Testament. What he made of classical mythology will just be touched on in chapters one and three.

13. Thomas and Roques, p. 434.
14. Paulin Paris, *Les MSS françois de la Bibliothèque du Roi* (Paris, 1846), 6:343–6; Thomas and Roques, p. 467; Louis Moland, *Origines littéraires de la France* (Paris, 1862), p. 276.

A fourth early translation, one which Antoine Thomas studied in detail, is to be found only in Vatican Library MS lat. 4788 (copied in 1309) and in a later retranslation into Latin (Thomas IV).[15] The work is contemporary with the version made by Jean de Meun (ca. 1305), and it is interesting to compare its author, one Pierre de Paris, with his illustrious compatriot, Jean. The comparison does not reflect credit on Pierre, however, who discharged his office of purveyor of culture to the Hospitallers of St. John of Jerusalem on the island of Cyprus in an aggressively ignorant fashion. During his residence on the island he composed two works now lost: a French translation of Aristotle's *Politics,* and a philosophical treatise dedicated to Amauri de Lusignan. His surviving works consist of the translation of the *Consolatio* and a French paraphrase of the Psalter with a commentary drawn largely from the *Glossa ordinaria.* His language shows him to be a non-Frenchman, possibly from the Dalmatian coast, who thought he had acquired enough French, island Greek, and school Latin to bring the classics to the Hospitallers.

Pierre seems to have been commissioned to supply an unnamed patron with this glossed translation of the *Consolatio.* Not only was the task in many ways beyond his capacities, however; he also apparently labored under the additional handicap of having no immediately available secondary sources. It is for exactly this reason that his work is of particular interest in the present study. Whereas every other translation considered here can be shown to have clear relations with some other translation or commentary, Pierre's work was created in a virtual vacuum. It is all the more remarkable that he shows not the slightest reticence in displaying his ignorance. He insists, in fact, on annotating all but a few of the philosophical distinctions and rhetorical allusions in the Boethian text. To support his conclusions he drew not only on his quite personal view of Aristotelianism but on folklore and homely *contes.* His translation will provide, in consequence, some of the most effective examples of medievalization to be pondered in the final chapter.

Because of the renown of its author as well as its intrinsic merit, the medieval translation of the *Consolatio* made by Jean de Meun (the only one to have been printed since the sixteenth century) has been intensively studied (Thomas III, Delisle I). The authorship of this lean, prose version was indisputably established by Ernest Langlois in 1913, and an excellent

---

15. Antoine Thomas, "Notice sur le MS. 4788 du Vatican," *Notices et extraits de MSS de la Bibliothèque Nationale* 41 (1917):29–90. Prints extensive selections.

edition based on seventeen MSS was published in 1952 by V. L. Dedeck-Héry.[16] Although Jean's version contains no examples of the kind of narrative elaboration that justifies this study, his is the first version to show a clear awareness of the roles played by the basic fictional personae of the *Consolatio,* Boethius and Lady Philosophy:

> Boeces establist et represente soi en partie de homme troublé et tourmenté et demené par passions sensibles et establist Philosophie en partie de homme elevé et ensuivant les biens entendibles. Si que en la partie de soy il demonstre ses douleurs et les causes qui ses douleurs esmeuvent, et en la partie de Philosophie il amene les causes qui aneantissent ses douleurs et demonstre le confort qui l'oste de ses douleurs. Et por ce est apeléz cist livres *Li Livres de Confort de Philosophie.* Si que deux personnes sont ici senefiées, c'est a savoir li malades et li mires.[17]

I mentioned at the beginning of this survey that the chief deterrent to the popularity of the first four prose versions of the *Consolatio* was that they were dialectally offcenter and, in two cases, intellectually aberrant. With the advent of Jean de Meun's close and intelligent translation, both of these problems were solved. It was at this point that the processes of manuscript transmission could take over in refining and adapting Jean's text to a variety of audiences. Because Jean's version was frequently copied, it shared the general fate of handmade literature to pass from scribe to scribe, from copyist to remanieur, from redactor to compiler, from plagiarist to recensor; and successive texts preserve the results of their handiwork. Discriminating some of the characteristic literary effects of these manuscript processes will be the secondary interest of this study, because such revision can provide clues to the comtemporary interpretation of works from an age which lacks more overt forms of literary self-evaluation.

One of these processes is compilation, and, because I will be making little use of Jean's version in the remainder of this study of narratives, I will cite him here as an example of this process. One of Jean's successors, as we shall see, simply borrowed Jean's prologue and affixed it to his own

---

16. Ernest Langlois, "La Traduction de Boèce par Jean de Meun," *Romania* 42 (1913):331–69; Dedeck–Héry's edition (see note 5) missed one MS: Paris, Arsenal 738, which appears to be in the tradition of his inferior branch *b*.

17. Dedeck–Héry, edition, p. 171. See comment on this passage in Peter Dronke's review of Courcelle in *Speculum* 44 (1969):127.

revision of someone else's prose-and-verse translation. Two MSS (B. N. fr. 809 and Arsenal 2669) indicate that a successor to all of the above persons compiled a version using a revised dedicatory epistle, Jean's prose translation of the meters, and the proses of the mixed version. Another scribe, Matthias Rivalli, addressed himself, ca. 1355–62, specifically to the problem of the audience when he justified his substitution of Jean's prose for the text of the mixed version from Book V, prose 3 forward, in these words: "Jusque cy souffist par tant comme il en appartient aus *lais,* et depuis ci jusques a la fin a esté pris de la translacion que fist maistre Jehan de Meun et est trop fort a entendre se n'est a *gens bien lettrez*" (MS Dijon 525).[18]

Between the making of Jean de Meun's translation and that of Renaut de Louhans in 1336–7, a yet anonymous author attempted a sixth version of the *Consolatio,* which sought formal faithfulness by matching prose to prose and verse to verse (Thomas V, Delisle III). This version marks the beginning of vernacular attention to the *Consolatio* as a literary masterpiece with forms worth imitating. As the translator says in his brief introduction:

> Ou livre a vers et s'i a prose:
> Si vueil si ordonner la chose
> Que li vers soient mis en rime
> Ou consonant ou leolime;
> La prose est mise plainnement.

This version, which survives in four MSS, was composed in the dialect of Lorraine, and, although less exact than Jean de Meun's translation, remains closely bound to the model text. It attempts no interpolations, either of doctrine or narrative. For our purposes the most interesting thing about the text is the use made of it by Renaut, an anonymous revisor, and a subsequent glossator.

On the basis of this mixed translation from Lorraine, a seventh version was made, and it became the most popular of all medieval versions, for its two states survive in a total of fifty-one MSS, and these MSS, more than those of any other version, tend to be very handsome and costly productions (Thomas VI, Delisle II). It is not too difficult to determine the reasons for its success. For one thing, its audacious maker simply lifted the proheme of Jean de Meun's version with its dedication to Philippe

18. Thomas and Roques, p. 438; Dedeck–Héry, "The MSS," p. 436.

le Bel and attached it to his own revision of the mixed prose-and-verse translation from Lorraine just described. I find this first state represented in only four MSS in the Bibliothèque Nationale: fr. 1728, 1948, 24231, and the fragmentary nouv. acq. fr. 20001. Fully as germane to its popularity is the fact that most MSS of this revised translation contain an extensive intertextual commentary, derived from William of Conches. This second state is represented by the remaining sixteen MSS of this version in the Bibliothèque Nationale.

The author of the commentary and the revisor of the original mixed version were different persons. This is apparent not only from the fact that some MSS lack the glosses. Where Boethius wrote in Book II, meter 7, of the bones of Fabricius, this revised mixed version asks: "Ou sont ore les os Platon?" But the gloss explains: "Note chi que la ou il dit ichi Platon, l'acteur du latin dit Fabricius, consul de Romme, et fut mout vaillant homme."[19] These successive authors, then, achieved the most attractive package of the *Consolatio,* adding the authority of Jean de Meun's name, rectifying rimes and clarifying allusions, and appending glosses to explain away Boethian mysteries. This text was printed in Lyon in 1483, 1485–90, and 1507, and in Paris in 1520.[20]

Four medieval French translations of the *Consolatio* are wholly in verse, all of them, I believe, postdating the prose versions. Sometime after the famine of 1315, to which he alludes, and before 1382, when the earliest surviving MS was copied, a very prolific poet served up an obviously digressive 12,300-line version of Boethius (Thomas VII, Delisle IV).[21] This translation exists complete in one MS, B. N. fr. 576, and fragmentarily in another, B. N. fr. 1543. Of its author, only the birthplace—Meun—is known. Although this eighth version is interesting from several points of view, it will be discussed most extensively in chapter 3 as one of the more extreme attempts to integrate material from the Latin mythographies, commentaries, and encyclopedias into a verse *Roman de philosophie.*

Another verse translation was completed by Frère Renaut de Louhans, a Dominican from Poligny (Jura), in 1336 or 1337 (Thomas IX, Delisle VII). Renaut's poem is also heavily digressive, in ways quite differ-

19. See Ernest Langlois, *Romania,* p. 347.
20. Full descriptions of the first two can be found in the *Gesamtkatalog der Wiegendrucke,* 4 (Leipzig, 1930), nos. 4577–8.
21. For its philosophical content, see C. V. Langlois, *Vie en France,* 4:294–302.

ent from the version by the Anonymous of Meun. It makes use of the first mixed version, as well as the commentary on the *Consolatio* by Renaut's fellow Dominican, Nicholas Trevet. This ninth translation, extant in over thirty MSS, was revised at least twice and one of the revisions was in turn reworked. There is additional evidence of its popularity in the possibility that Villon may have known of it and that Pierre Salmon, a Burgundian agent at the court of Charles VI, worked extracts from it into a version of his rambling *Demandes* addressed to the king.[22] The narratives of Renaut's version, notable for their lack of explicit moralization, provide examples for the discussion of the translators' use of history in chapter 2, and his prosodic experiments and fund of popular tales round out the matter of the final chapter.

Around 1380 Renaut's version of the *Consolatio* was revised by an as yet anonymous author who, according to the epilogue extant only in MS Toulouse 822, had a busy career (Delisle VIII). Born in Picardy, he became a Benedictine monk, served as a Prior in Savoy and, as he reveals, sat at the table of Louis II of Bourbon, count of Clermont in Beauvaisis.[23] His revision, which was apparently as popular as Renaut's original, is prefaced by a 150-line prologue detailing his intentions. He says he has read a bad prose translation (Bonaventura's?) which dwelt on the fables and skipped long passages, "com oysel sur festus," and he learned too late of a good "extrait" of the *Consolatio* in verse made by one Jean de Cis.[24] The Benedictine's translation was dismissed by Mario Roques as being only "un démarquage, avec élimination des provincialismes et rectification des rimes, de la traduction de Renaud de Louhans."[25] The Benedictine himself says nothing of Renaut, however, and his work is in fact more original than Roques allows, some of its verses, like that on the Golden Age (Book II, meter 5), being entirely original, and many scholarly qualifications being made on what he left of Renaut. This version was printed in Geneva before 1481.[26]

22. See the present author's "Villon's Boethius," *Annuale Medievale* 11 (1970): 74–80. The Boethian translations are not recognized as Renaut's in either of the editions of Salmon: *Les Demands faites par le roi Charles VI,* ed. G. A. Crapelet (Paris, 1833), or that in J. A. Buchon, ed., *Collection des chroniques* (Paris, 1827), vol. 25.
23. See C. V. Langlois, *Vie en France,* 4:293.
24. Ibid., p. 291.
25. Thomas and Roques, p. 488.
26. *Gesamtkatalog,* 4, no. 4581.

The translation in MS B. N. fr. 25418, from the end of the fourteenth century—the eleventh version to be noted here—has been mentioned in the surveys from Gröber to Roques as an abbreviation of the Benedictine's version (Delisle VI). It is nothing of the kind, sharing, in fact, only a few miscellaneous lines with that version. It is, rather, a skillful though anti-intellectual condensation of Renaut's translation, omitting, for example, all of the philosophical arguments of Book V. Another curious MS, B. N. fr. 12459, is a unique compilation of the translations by Renaut and the Benedictine, and does not need to be accorded the status of an independent version. One of its concoctions is discussed in the last chapter.

More interesting than either of these MSS is a second mixed version in prose and verse, preserved uniquely in National Library of Wales MS 5038.[27] The verses represent a slight revision of the Benedictine's revision, but the proses are more original and seem to be a kind of updated epitome of Jean de Meun's prose. The chief interest the MS offers for the present study lies in the stylistic refinement to which an otherwise acceptable vernacular Boethius has been subjected. By the beginning of the fifteenth century the doctrinal problems had been ironed out and the canonical fables selected; only polishing remained.

Less has been published about the thirteenth and last medieval French version of the *Consolatio* than about any of the others. It is in mixed verse and prose and appears, mingled with an anonymous translation of the commentary of Regnier de Saint Trond, in a print issued by Colard Mansion in Bruges in 1477 and reissued with an added preface by Antoine Verard in Paris, 1494.[28] On the basis of an indication in the colophon that the translation was finished the same day Mansion printed the book, it has been conjectured that the translation may have been made by Mansion himself.[29] I think there is better evidence that it was not. On the occasion of the presentation of a collection of Mansion's printings to the city of Bruges in 1837, a local notable read a paper in which he had collected a list of Flemish dialecticisms from Mansion's MSS.[30] I find

27. First described by the present author in "Another Boece," *Romance Philology* 19 (1965):268–70.
28. *Gesamtkatalog*, 4, nos. 4579–80.
29. Patch, *Tradition*, p. 154.
30. Count F. A. de Muelenaere, *Discours . . . des editions de Colard Mansion* (Bruges, 1837).

none of these words in the translation of the *Consolatio.* Furthermore, the translator's prologue contains some highly sophisticated language for a printer: "la forme du sillogisme precedent est prouvé par le tiers meus de la premier figure sillogistique qu'on appelle *darii.* Le mineur peut estre declarée par la maniere comme le maieur & ce quant a toutes ses parties." In any event, this version is quite interesting for the experimental fashion in which the author attempted to match the diversity of Boethian metrics.

Having come through these necessary preliminaries, we repeat that the prime focus of the discussion to follow is literary, that we are always concerned with the meaning and aesthetic effect which the many interpolated narratives generate in themselves and in their Boethian contexts. We will also attend to some consequences of these narratives having been submitted to the protean processes of manuscript transmission. The study thus uses the techniques of both the literary critic and the bibliographer to answer the literary historian's question: how do the best parts of these translations taken collectively exhibit aspects of the popular medieval uses of Boethius?[31]

31. All quotations from the *Consolatio* in this study are taken from *Boethius,* ed. and trans. H. F. Stewart and E. K. Rand, Loeb Classical Library (Cambridge, Mass.: Harvard Univ. Press, 1918), although I have checked them against the standard critical edition by Ludwig Bieler, *Boethii Philosophiae Consolatio,* Corpus Christianorum ser. lat. 94 (Turnhout, 1957).

I

The Earth Is Made
to Speak

*Et use l'acteur d'une maniere de parler que on dit poetique, c'est a
dire feinctive, de laquele les poetes anciens ont acoustumé a user
en leurs livres en disant et faignant que la terre parle et les autres
choses lesqueles naturelment sont mues.*[1]

A GREAT PART of the *Consolatio philosophiae* is, of course, devoted to
demonstrating through logical argument the truths of the Neoplatonic
view of the universe and man's place in it. The problems and challenges
this logical structure has given translators are the subject of F. Anne
Payne's work on the Old English version of the *Consolatio,* which shows
how King Alfred attempted to find in personal wisdom and the resources
of Old English syntax a non-logical alternative to the chain of proposi-
tions.[2] But syllogistic reasoning is only a part—I would say a neat half—of
the means by which Boethius tries to persuade us. In the course of the
Consolatio, principally in the verse passages, Boethius resorts to mythological exempla in the careers of Ulysses, Orpheus, Hercules, and their
satellites; to rhetorical allusion to such natural entities as the winds
(Auster, Boreas, Corus) and the rivers (Euripus, Hermus, Indus), and to
many other personifications and places from Tartarus to Thule. In addition, Boethius calls on human history—almost exclusively pre-Christian—
for some forty illustrations from the lives of real persons from Aemilius
Paulus to Zeno the Eleatic. The medieval French translators were fascinated by these allusions, and very few of them took King Alfred's course
of substituting a familiar name like Weland the Smith for a stranger like
Fabricius. Instead, they tended to resort to narrative dilation of the brief
Boethian notices, with the result that we are provided with a rich vein of

1. Proheme to revised mixed version. Quoted from Nat. Lib. of Wales MS 5039,
   fols. 4–4v.
2. F. Anne Payne, *King Alfred and Boethius* (Madison, 1969).

evidence from which to mine non-discursive medieval interpretations of the late classical argument that is their matrix.

One place to begin is with a consideration of what these allusions and exempla meant to Boethius. And because most of them occur in the verses, a prior question should be what the use of verse itself meant to Boethius. Both H. F. Stewart and Pierre Courcelle, to take an older and a recent authority, concur in observing that, except for the basic notion of a medley of prose and verse, Boethius owed little to the earlier uses of *satura* by Menippus of Gadara (fl. 60 B.C.) or Terentius Varro, the younger Seneca (in his *Apocolacyntosis Claudii*), Petronius Arbiter, or even Martianus Capella, who wrote but a hundred years before him. Stewart observes that whereas Boethius's forerunners

> had heedlessly jumbled prose and verse, falling into the latter sometimes in the very middle of a sentence, he is careful to balance nicely the one against the other, choosing the moment with consummate art for the insertion of a song which shall carry on, and give emphasis to, the thoughts on which he has already exercised the full force of his pedestrian rhetoric and logical argument.
>
> The regular appearance of poetry in the midst of a prose that (to us at least) is always difficult and sometimes dry, was doubtless intended to serve a double purpose: in the first place, to relieve the strain on the writer, without sensibly lowering the tone of the dialogue; and secondly, to refresh the reader with a constant and agreeable variety.[3]

Courcelle has this to say about what Boethius does and does not take from *satura*: "Enfin Boèce a pris à la satire l'usage d'introduire des sentences ou proverbes grecs, à titre d'ornements, dans sa prose. Au reste, Boèce doit peu au genre de la satire; car c'est lui-même qui a rendu cette alternance de prose et de vers régulière; et il refuse une loi du genre, qui admettait le cynisme et l'obscénité."[4] Later I shall discuss the medieval practice in relation to this last law, but here I may conclude this glance at authority by calling attention to the remark of Richard H. Green, a careful modern translator of the *Consolatio,* that Boethius seems to concur in the medieval estimate of poetry as one of the lower arts ancillary to dialectic when he alludes to the use of verse as rest and refreshment. But against this view of the basically ornamental function of the verses—ostensibly Boethius's own

<hr>

3. H. F. Stewart, *Boethius: An Essay* (Edinburgh, 1891), p. 76.
4. Pierre Courcelle, *La Consolation de philosophie dans la tradition littéraire* (Paris, 1967), p. 17.

view—Green opposes the "profound syntheses of the philosophical impli-
cations" and the "astonishing poetic concentration and power" of such
verses as Book I, meter 5, and III, meter 9.[5]

The near-contradiction in these various comments is that their authors
see the verses as secondary in importance to the prose discussion at the
same time as they would claim for them an artistic status at least equal
with that of the prose. This is, in fact, the view which is also implicit in the
prefatory comments by the thirteenth-century author of the earliest
French translation of the *Consolatio,* who noted that Boethius "fait vint e
set manieres de metres que par la dolçor e la diversité del chant de musique
conforte la dolor de la persone dolente. La plus grant partie del livre est
faite par prose, quar Boece ne fu menor de Tulle en prose, ne Vergile en
metre."[6] And on the same subject, the version printed by Colard Mansion
in 1477 is only more academic and more lyrical: "Cestui acteur en forme
poeticque a ensuivi Marcian l'eureux, lequel avoit ainsi par metre et par
prose escript le livre des *Nopces Philologie,* comme Alain en son livre qu'il
fist de la *Complainte de Nature* a ensuivi Boece. Maintenant nostre acteur
monstre et fait chansons metrifiéez melodieuses pour soy souevement
deliciter, maintenant il soubzjoinct proses pesantes et sentencieuses pour
soy informer."

A higher intellectual status for Boethius's verses and their rhetorical
matter may reasonably be claimed, however, than any ventured by the
authors cited above. The emphasis on refreshment as the function of
Boethius's poetry, for example, arises only if we focus on those verses in
which Philosophy herself is the speaker. Of course all the verse and prose is
directed at our, the audience's, delight and instruction, but in terms of the
dramatic framework of the *Consolatio* not all of the poems have the same
audience. Four of them are sung by the narrating Boethius, and when we
look at these verses we can better see the range of non-discursive, and
non-refreshing, uses of poetry. Book I, meter 1, is a *complaint* made up of
intimate personal details—"Intempestiui funduntur uertice cani / Et tremit
effeto corpore laxa cutis" (11–12)—to which are added sententious
observations—"Qui cecidit, stabili non erat ille gradu" (22). But these
verses lack rational explanation of the connection between the narrator's
prematurely grey hair and his longstanding insecurity. Meter 3 is an *epic*

5. *The Consolation of Philosophy,* trans. Richard Green (Indianapolis, 1962), pp.
   xx–xxi.
6. MS Vienna 2642, fol. 1v.

simile, comparing Boethius's drying his eyes to the work of one wind in sweeping away the overcast brought by another and revealing "uibratus lumine Phoebus" (9). Meter 5 is, of course, the great *prayer* offered by Boethius, "O stelliferi conditor orbis," which consists of directly addressed petitions, abstract questions, moral judgments, and classical allusions. Finally, Book V, meter 3, is an extension of Boethius's claim in the preceding prose that divine foreknowledge and free human will are incompatible, but the verse is syntactically distinguished from the prose by a rich use of *rhetorical questions*—ten in thirty lines. Additionally, one poem, Book II, meter 2, is delivered by Philosophy in the persona of Fortune and in the *subjunctive mood* on the topic of man's insatiable greed should even an ideal largess prevail. In these five varieties of discourse—and there are others—we can see some of the ways in which verses clearly not intended to refresh anyone are linguistically and functionally distinguished from the prose. In function the prose is restricted to rational dialectic, with the form limited to catechism, syllogism, and dialogue, none of which are to be found in the verses. The verses might be said, then, to constitute modes of knowing and discoursing alternative to those central to speculative philosophy, and this is a far cry from diverting decoration or even what Sir Philip Sidney called "a medicine of cherries."

Boethius himself tells us (Book V, prose 4) that rational argument is only an intermediate stage in the levels of awareness from brute sensation to an intelligence of divine order. These levels constitute a spatial metaphor, but Boethius also uses a temporal metaphor that can be related to his use of poetic mythology. This temporal metaphor arises from his allegiance to the Platonic doctrine of reminiscence: "Quod quisque discit immemor recordatur" (Book III, meter 11, line 16). Remembering the truth is not the same as discovering it by syllogistic argument, and recalling the human past may be a temporal analogue to the spatial ascent to intelligence. Recollections of the pagan gods, heroes, and great men who form the myth of the past constitute a succession of flashbacks in human time which collectively mirror truth as it rests in eternity, where all events are perceived by the Boethian God as simultaneous. Although we cannot foresee the future, the more we remember of the past, the more like God we can become. This reminiscence has a practical use too. In the archetypical behavior of a Nero or a Hercules can be glimpsed patterns that organize the perplexing disorder that involves men here and now, and these poetic glimpses take their legitimate place in alternation with the conclusions at which reason arrives. History and myth are as true, then, as a syllogism is true, but their vehicle is more properly verse just as the most proper vehicle of the syllogism is prose. And the proper linguistic expression of the ultimate intelligence of timeless, spaceless divine order may be neither of these, but rather the laughter of a Troilus in the eighth sphere.

Although Boethius's prose and verse are linguistically distinguished to some extent as two modes of knowing and discoursing, the notion of reminiscence also shares something with that of abstract reasoning. Just as the conclusion to a syllogism is implicit in its premises, just so the ultimate object of each chain of reminiscence is already contained in the memory. The function of allusion is to set the memory going, turning over its riches until the desired truth is reclaimed. A highly developed poetry of allusion is essentially non-narrative inasmuch as the narrative links are left to be supplied by the memories and imaginations of all those initiated into the rhetorical arcana. Not surprisingly, the men who translate such a poetry for an uninitiated audience will be moved to reconstruct the suppressed narrative links, on the score that such details will be unfamiliar to this new audience. The following discussion will focus on two aspects of this task: how the translators went about filling in the gaps, and what their narrative additions tell us about the medieval interpretation of Boethian allusions.

When we turn from the late classical milieu that governed Boethian rhetoric to the medieval French versions of the *Consolatio,* we find that the diversity of the translators' responses to the allusions mirrors much of the range of other late medieval usage of the past—a range which I take to extend from the incidental adducing of antique example to the enthusiastic and encyclopedic amassing of genuine and spurious classical lore for assimilation into such works as Raoul Lefevre's *Le Recueil des hystoires de Troyes* (1464). We shall see, for example, that certain of the translators worked in a near vacuum, and a dark one at that. Here, Jean de Meun's refusal to extend the letter of the Boethian text must be contrasted with the simple ignorance of myth shown by the authors of the Wallonian prose version and, to a lesser extent, the first mixed version. Others, such as Bonaventura da Demena and Pierre de Paris, aggressively amplified their translations on the basis of homely religious or secular materials and fearless misinterpretations. In contrast with all these, such translators as the author of the Burgundian prose version and the glossator of the revised mixed version will be seen to have bound their work closely to the explications of myth and history available in the great Latin commentaries on the

Consolatio—although their borrowings differ considerably as they are made early or late.

Still other translators, Renaut de Louhans and the Anonymous of Meun, for example, bear interesting though differing resemblances to the commentators described by Beryl Smalley as classicizers of the English mendicant sort.[7] Finally, the work of Renaut and his revisors manifests both the effects of new principles of narrative experimentation for its own sake and later reactions to that freedom as adaptors retain, alter, and reject aspects of their predecessors' elaborations. But the chief lesson of the translations is always to be sought in their tendency to medievalize the *Consolatio* in popular ways unavailable to the Latin commentators and to do so in a straightforward fashion uncomplicated by the ulterior purposes of higher art forms. Additionally, it will be seen that the illustrators of manuscripts of the translations reflected in their own medium quite parallel medievalizing tendencies.

The Boethian uses of mythology and human history fascinated the vernacular translators for reasons doubtlessly far removed from those governing their original creation. But even while the doctrine of reminiscence was not available to guarantee a serious reception for the allusive passages, such passages tended to become the chief attraction, especially in the work of those translators who versified the whole of the *Consolatio*. The reasons for this interest in storytelling will become apparent, I hope, as I proceed, but this summary will begin with those few translators who, employing no secondary aids to their reading, made little or nothing or worse of Boethius's rich banquet of allusions. The translators' decisions about verse form will be explored in Chapter Four.

Part of the translators' problem in dealing adequately with Boethian mythology and history was that, precisely because it represented a form of knowledge, it possessed an arcane aspect. Like mathematics to a Pythagorean, it was lore for the initiated. No one, of course, could be expected to identify such minor Goths and Romans as Conigastus and Trigula, Canius and Papinianus, but the truly embarrassing difficulty lay elsewhere. In meter 3 of Book IV, for example, Boethius calls up Circe's enchantment of the crew of Ulysses to illustrate the natural bestiality of sinful men. But in this passage, Ulysses is identified only as *Neritii ducis*, Circe as *pulchra*

7. Beryl Smalley, *English Friars and Antiquity in the Early Fourteenth Century* (Oxford, 1960).

dea, and Mercury as *Arcadis alitis.* In such a fog, the unaided translators struck out on a variety of courses. None of them was so extreme as the Anglo-Norman adaptor, Simund de Freine, who simply eliminated all mythological and historical references. The closest to Simund among the translators is the anonymous author of the Wallonian prose version, who eliminated some proper names and simply misread others. His version of the Orpheus passage (Book III, meter 12) correctly identified the hero but omitted any direct mention of the names Eurydice, Thrace, Taenarus, Ixion, Tantalus, Tityus, Tartara, as well as allusions to Cerberus and the Furies, all to be found there. In his version of the poem on the Golden Age (Book II, meter 5), he neglected any attempt at the forms *Bacchica, Serum,* and *Tyrio,* although *ignibus Aetnae* is rendered as *feu d'infier.* Finally, in Book I, prose 3, the translator made several alterations, giving Zeno as *Tonon,* Seneca as *Seneton,* and Canius as *Kamost.*

The work of the Sicilian, Bonaventura da Demena, represents a slightly higher stage in the confrontation of this mysterious lore; for while he missed many names and misread others, he refused to shrink from the task of providing *some* narrative when the text seemed to be calling for it.[8] His labors have been rewarded with the following comments by Antoine Thomas: "Quand [il] 'imite,' il lui arrive trop souvent, par manque de goût, de 'travestir'," and "Il a cru faire oeuvre pie en versant le christianisme dans la *Consolatio,* n'ayant pas assez de sens littéraire pour s'apercevoir que c'était une sorte de profanation."[9] The animus for this abuse can be seen, for instance, in Bonaventura's typical failure to recognize Ulysses and Circe in the passage we have been discussing: "Il fu jadis un home qi avoit nom Naracie. Cist Naracie, por aler en une soe besoigne, se mist com sa maisnie au chemins de la mer, mais la Fortune et la tempeste et le grand vent de la mer le menerent outre son gré en une isle de une dame qi estoit fee."[10]

Extenuating next to nothing, the translator of the first mixed version correctly apprehended more names than any of the translators considered so far, omitted some, and altered or explained by circumlocution a few others. From the verse on the Golden Age, for example, he omitted all

8. His version of the Orpheus legend has a certain notoriety. See the commentators mentioned in note 14 to the Introduction.
9. Antoine Thomas and Mario Roques, "Traductions françaises de la *Cons. Phil.* de Boèce," in *Hist. litt. de la France* (Paris, 1938), 37:467–8.
10. MS B. N. fr. 821, fol. 43v.

proper names, but in Book IV, meter 7, he rendered Hercules, Cerberus, Achelous, and Evander closely enough, and helpfully gave for *Centauros,* "les gens qui sont demis chevaulz," and for *Hydra,* "serpent." But *Cacus* became *Cathon* for whatever use the reader could make of it. Occasionally the translator yielded to a popularizing impulse, as when he rendered *Arcturus* as the *char Saint Martin*; but here he was rescued by his revisor who turned that reading into *Septentrion* and corrected his misinterpretation of that troublesome *Neritii ducis* as Hercules. The work of the glossator of this revised mixed version will be discussed in connection with the uses other translators made of the formal mythological glosses of William of Conches and Nicholas Trevet.

But it is time to leave these amateurs behind and turn to the translators who were more successful and more systematic in responding to Boethian allusion. To structure the basic discussion of this and the next two chapters, I will draw on a distinction which was made by William of Conches and was taken with varying seriousness by several of the French translators and manuscript illustrators. In his gloss on Book IV, meter 7, William observed that such stories as those of Agammemnon, Ulysses, and Hercules teach us by three methods: *"Bella bis quinis*: Quia dixerat sapientes cum omni fortuna bellum conserere, ad illud prelium hortatur nos in istis versibus tribus modis: per historiam, per integumentum, deinde ponendo premia que sequuntur."[11] And one MS of the glosses adds a fourth mode: *per fabulam.* It is on such a distinction that the translator of the earliest French version of the *Consolatio* drew when he prefaced his comments on the legend of Orpheus with these remarks: "Nos devons saveir que li demonstrementz des auctors e des philosofes est feite par treis manieres: par fables, o par estoires, o par integument. Fable si est chose feinte semblant de veir, ausi come fait Ovides. Hystoire si est chose feite recontee issi come ele fu feite. Integumentz est quant om dit une chose e senefie autre, si come est ici de Orpheo."[12]

In the case of both William of Conches and his French translator, we have here a technical *topos* of medieval exegesis that did not find much other expression in the bulk of vernacular versions of the Boethian text. As I hope to show in the course of my argument, the translators became so attracted to the narrative possibilities of the allusions before them that

11. Quoted by Édouard Jeauneau, " 'Integumentum' chez Guillaume de Conches,"
    Archives d'histoire doctrinale et littéraire du moyen âge 24 (1957):37.
12. MS Vienna 2642, fols. 52–52v.

they ransacked the commentaries, the encyclopedias, and even their store of popular lore for fictions that would enliven their translations. The three-way distinction made by William of Conches is useful to me for the purpose of sorting out the kinds of narratives that the translators added to their versions, but it should be kept in mind that I am definitely not arguing that the translators intended their narrative elaborations to teach on various "levels." I do claim, however, that their stories may indirectly gloss Boethian ideas, with results that are sometimes so profoundly at variance with the original text that they can be said to "medievalize" it by making it, for example, *historial* as they spell out the adventures of Hercules or the matter of Orpheus, or sententious and pious as they retail the ten commandments or a long ballade on death, or thematically medieval in their appeal to Fortune's Wheel, the Seven Deadly Sins, or *fin amor*.

At this point in the discussion I want to show that this basic division between stories, whether true or false, on the one hand and allegories on the other is paralleled in the iconography associated with manuscripts of the translations, and I want to show a couple of the unexpected consequences of the translators' use of fable pure. The next chapter will take up the translators' use of history, while Chapter III will explore in detail what the commentators and translators made of the term "integument."

The evidence on Boethian iconography is drawn from the extensive discussion in Pierre Courcelle's study,[13] although I have seen in the original MSS all of the illustrations I mention. Courcelle's remarks need to be supplemented with the information that fully half of his illustrations are drawn from texts of translations of the *Consolatio*. He nowhere mentions this, in keeping with his exclusion of any consideration of vernacular versions from his commentary. This happily gives me the opportunity to make what I think is an important connection between the art of the translators and that of the miniaturists.

Medieval manuscript illustrations of the *Consolatio* can be usefully divided into those which depict narrative episodes and those which present static allegorical tableaux, with the former quite outnumbering the latter. For this discussion I shall limit myself to examples from two MSS representing the extremes in this distinction. MS 12, Trinity Hall Library, Cambridge, is a well-known, thickly illustrated volume whose curiosities

13. Op. cit.

have been noticed not only by Courcelle but by M. R. James, Astrik Gabriel, and myself.[14] The artist, working hastily but from excellent models according to James, sketched over 200 action-filled little scenes which convert even metaphors into narratives. Thus, on the mention of those philosophic sects which opposed Boethius's beloved Neoplatonism, we see a miniature of several brutes ripping the garments of a stately lady, and Boethius's defense of Paulinus from the *Palatinae canes* shows real dogs leaping at the Consul (fig. 1). But the artist's conception of Ulysses' sojourn on Circe's isle is probably most useful for the contrast I am making. Folio 60 of the Cambridge MS shows three scenes from the narrative (fig. 2). On the left are three swine munching acorns—the transmuted companions of Ulysses. Above right Mercury is shown handing to Ulysses the protective herb moly, and below we see Ulysses, now educated, vigorously refusing Circe's offer of food and drink. These scenes are realistic, the latter two seeming to be glimpsed through open windows.

With these representations let us compare some of the elegant miniatures in MS B. N. fr. 809. These beautiful half-page paintings are quite different in character from the sketches in the Trinity Hall MS. In the scene illustrating the Ulysses episode, we have clearly emblematic allegory (fig. 3).[15] Centered, before a background of trees and rocks, stands Philosophy. On either hand is a group of figures facing front. To the left stand several men, a woman, and Boethius, who modestly points to the crew on the right, a collection of beastheaded figures with human bodies and dress. Below, phylacteries bear the mysterious legends "Providence" and "Predestination," which Courcelle argues belong to a miniature at the head of Book IV. The scene, of course, illustrates no action from the appropriate meter, but rather a moral lesson implicit in it.

I will glance at just one other of the several illustrations in this MS worth calling attention to for their contrast with more narrative-based art. The interpretation of Fortune and her wheel is divided into two tableaux, and that on the left showing Philosophy consoling Boethius in prison is traditional (fig. 4).[16] At the doorway Fortune, with a double visage, calls

14. Courcelle, p. 196 and pl. 110 especially; Montague R. James, *A Descriptive Catalogue of the MSS in the Library of Trinity Hall, Cambridge* (Cambridge, 1907), pp. 14–32; Astrik Gabriel, "The Source of the Anecdote of the Inconstant Scholar," *Classica et Medievalia* 19 (1958):152–76; and R. A. Dwyer, " 'Je meurs de soif auprès de la fontaine,' " *French Studies* 23 (1969):225–8.
15. Courcelle, p. 196 and pl. 111.
16. Courcelle, p. 149 and pl. 78.

Figure 1. Boethius protects Paulinus from the *palatini canes*.
(Cambridge, Trinity Hall MS 12, fol. 7v)

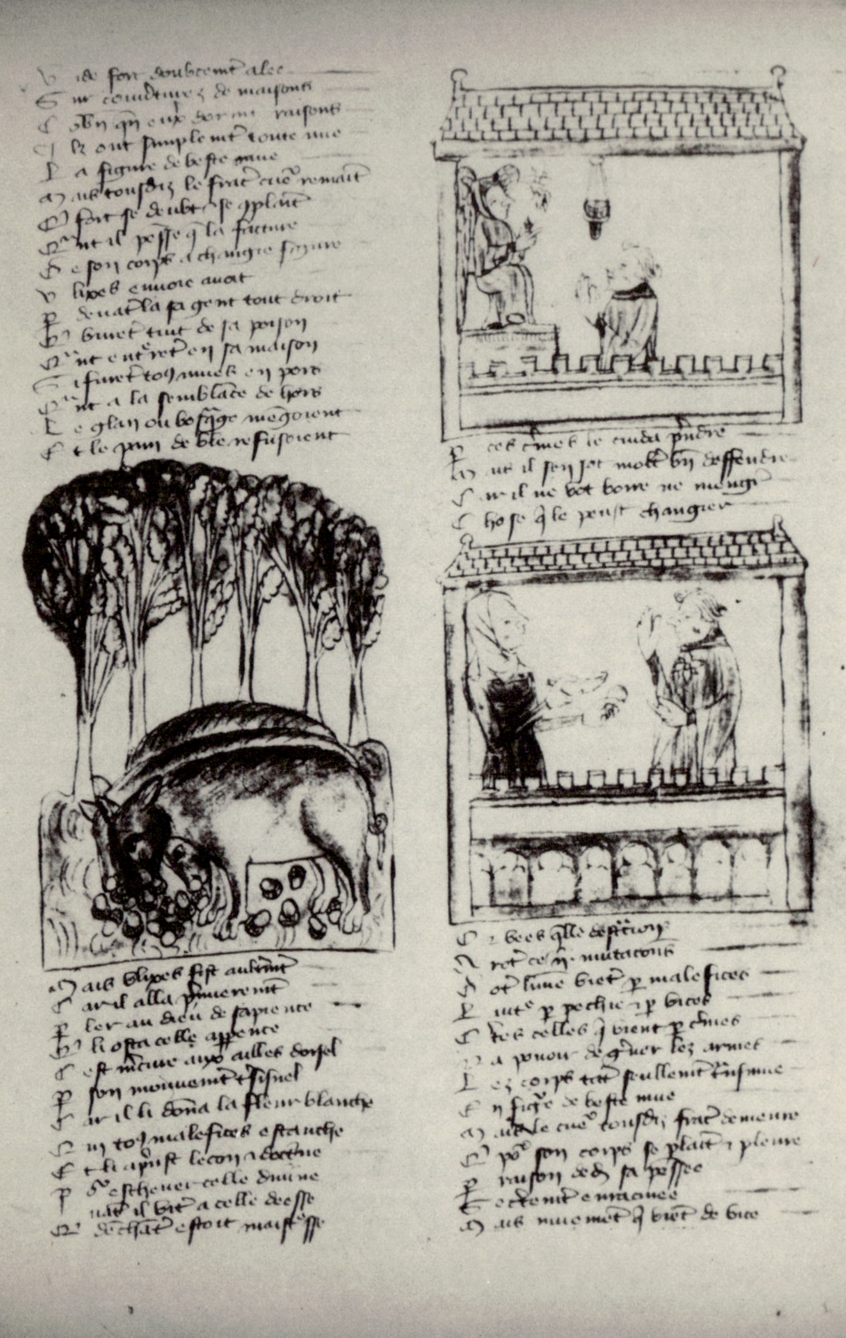

Figure 2.   Ulysses and Circe.
(Cambridge, Trinity Hall MS 12, fol. 60)

Figure 3. Circe and the transformed crew of Ulysses.
(B. N. MS fr. 809, fol. 67)

Figure 4.   Fortune's wheel and her goods.
(B. N. MS fr. 809, fol. 40)

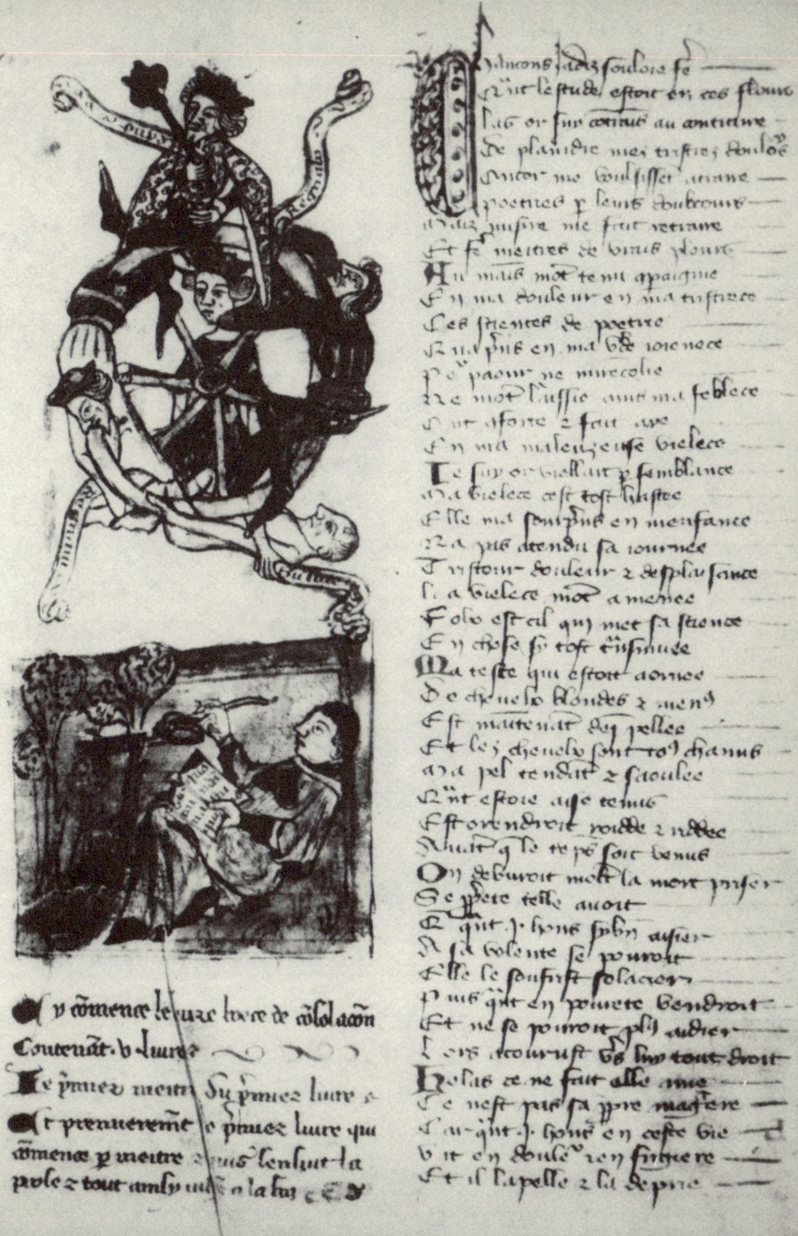

Figure 5.   Another wheel of fortune.
(Cambridge, Trinity Hall MS 12, fol. 3)

Et tant ot de fois auenture.
Que plaines en sont escriptures.
Et quant asses fut trauaillie.
Auec ses dieux fut essauee.
Asses donc ses fois par pser
Ou bon exemple vous adresce.
Et veez que ceulz vont requerir.
Le ciel. qui ont vincu la terre.

En ce quint liure de boece. determine
phie trois moult fortes questions nees
des choses dessusdictes. La pmiere est as
sauoir mon se cas ou aduenture est.
Cest adire se les choses de ce monde sont
ou auiennent de cas ou dauenture.
La seconde est se franc arbitraige cest
adire franche voulente homme est. La
tierce est. se franche voulete homme puet

Figure 6. The Ascent of Boethius.
(Rouen, Bibl. Mun. MS 3045, fol. 94)

on Boece to observe the wheel on the right. She extends her arms and thus links the two scenes. But we do not see the wheel turning and precipitating the powerful into adversity—as in the whirling scene in the Cambridge MS (fig. 5). Three personages are seated on chairs at the quarters of the wheel; a fourth sits between the upright supports of the wheel. The king is at the top, but on the left is a bourgeois holding a full purse, and on the right a young man beholds himself in a mirror. Below, a knight grasps a lance. The wheel thus shows the personified goods of Fortune: power, riches, beauty, and glory. The artist has combined in a static scene the two Boethian themes of the wheel and the gifts of Fortune.

The two approaches that we find in these MSS to making the Boethian message graphic are related to the sorts of translations which carry that message. The Cambridge MS is a text of the Benedictine's revision of Renaut de Louhans's verse translation. This version is, in fact, the least allegorized of those medieval French translations of the *Consolatio* that elaborate the text. In contrast to most of the other versions, the only moral it attaches to the Ulysses episode is that brief one written by Boethius himself. MS B. N. fr. 809, on the other hand, is a curious composite of Jean de Meun's prosing of Boethius's verses coupled with the glossed proses drawn from the revised mixed version. The moralizing glosses to the Ulysses episode, taken from William of Conches, run to over fifty lines in the MSS. There are thus parallels to be found in these MSS between the narrative techniques of the translators and the methods of illustrators as they opt for literal or allegorical paths to Boethian allusions.

Not many of the translators actually cited the three-way distinction among kinds of scholastic interpretation. But in the versions of the *Consolatio* by those translators whose narrative additions I will characterize as fable, history, or integument, it is the category of pure fable that least predominates. When the author of the earliest prose version, or Pierre de Paris, or the Anonymous of Meun related a classical fable, he generally strove to close it with a moralization in keeping with the methods of the Latin commentators. But occasionally he did not, and the resulting tales can be divided into two groups according to whether they are simply informative library exercises, or have some thematic relation, for better or worse, to the discursive matrix around them.

In the first category I would place such narrations as the eighty odd lines that the Anonymous Burgundian appended to the following innocent remark that Boethius let fall about Philosophy's logic-spinning: " 'Ludisne,' inquam, 'me inextricabilem labyrinthum rationibus texens' " (III, prose 12:82–3). To gloss this line, the Burgundian abandoned William of Conches's brief comment and amassed from the Vatican Mythographies a labyrinthine narration about Dedalus, the Minotaur, Icarus, and the romance of Theseus and Ariadne.[17] In the same spirit, but far less reliable in its scholarship, is the story of Jupiter and Io that Pierre de Paris was moved to add to Book IV, meter 1, apropos of Boethius's metaphor of the wings of Philosophy. It seems that the appearance in the fable of winged Mercury was the justification, although Pierre engages in some ingenious stretching of its relevance before falling flat with his concluding advice:

> Et dient les fables que celuy Mercurius fait descendre dou ciel la gelee. . . . Et por ce que par la influence de une estoyle, qui est molt resplendissable et qui blanchoie, vient le froit en les terres, si veut dire la Philosophie que auci celuy Mercurius est au ciel et est guyor de cele estoile, tout auci et celuy qui vodra aler en ciel si avra belles pennes et cleres et nettes et molt ligeres, par les queles il porra voler jusques au ciel.[18]

I find it demanding too great a leap of literary faith to picture Pierre smiling ironically over his advice that those who would fly to the heavens will need light, well-feathered wings for the trip.

The case is otherwise, however, with some of the unmoralized additions of the anonymous Burgundian author of the earliest translation. He has received high praise from Antoine Thomas for his intelligence and discrimination, and I am inclined to agree. In view of his intelligence, and the Dedalus example aside, it is wise to proceed with his elaborations on the assumption that he knew what he was doing with them. Two examples will be offered whose relation to the Boethian text exhibits in turn the virtue and vice of the eclectic methods of medieval art.

The first of these narratives occurs in the Burgundian's translation of prose 3 of the last book. There Boethius is discussing God's limitless foreknowledge, which he contrasts with man's puny ability to prophesy. In scornful illustration, he mentions the absurd prophecy of Tiresias: "Quid-

---

17. MS Vienna 2642, fols. 50–51v. For the source of this passage, see Georg H. Bode, *Scriptores rerum mythicarum latini tres* (Cellis, 1834), p. 94.

18. MS Vat. lat. 4788, fol. 69v. Cited also in Antoine Thomas, "Notice sur le MS. 4788 du Vatican," *Notices et extraits de MSS. de la Bibliothèque Nationale* 41 (1917):71.

quid dicam, aut erit aut non," which Boethius took from Horace's second *Satire*. At this point all of the major commentaries tell the story of Tiresias's seeing the copulating snakes and his unsatisfactory answer to a question of Juno's. Here is how the Burgundian tells it:

> Jupiter e Juno soperent un seir ensemble, e aprés le vin parlerent de deduit. Juno dist que li hom esteit plus luxuries que la femme. Jupiter dist non. Il plot a ambedous oïr le jugement de Tyresias, car il aveit esté home e femme. En tel maniere il vit dous serpenz ajoster ensemble e devint femme; autre feitz les vit ajoster e redevint home, car li serpent esteient de tel nature. Jupiter e Juno vindrent devant lui. Tyresias juja que la femme aveit .ix. tant de luxure que li hom. Juno fu corrocee, si li traist les iouz; Jupiter li otroia que fust devineor e que seüst ce que esteit avenir.[19]

Oddly enough, after relating this same anecdote, the Latin commentary edited by E. T. Silk remarks, "Ista autem fabula ad hunc Boetii sermonem non pertinet."[20] The commentator may be wrong, for the fable has arguable ironic relevance to Boethius's message. Tiresias was cited in the first place because of the pathetic equivocation of his prophecy. The anecdote told above shows what enormous lack of real foresight he used in acquiring his weak gift by venturing lightly considered judgments in the company of Juno, and it further alludes to the experience he gained as a whore after first seeing the snakes—surely no confirmation of his credibility. By contrast with this rueful pagan story of divine toying with man's faculties, the Christian God's benevolence and infinite certainty are clearly enhanced.

The final example in this section is taken from the gloss to Boethius's remark in Book IV, meter 6, that the constellation *Ursa major* never sets beneath the waves.[21] Calixto, one of Diana's chaste company, had the misfortune to catch the eye of Jupiter, who confronted her alone in the woods. "Jupiter li rendi sun salu dolcement, e en rïant si l'embracea, si la baisa e la traist pres de sei, e mostra li qu'il esteit Jupiter; car il jut a li, e ele conceut un enfant. Aprés long tens, Dïana conut e vit que ele esteit grosse, si la geta de sa compaignie." Calixto named her new child Arcas.

---

19. MS Vienna 2642, fol. 81.
20. Edmund T. Silk, ed., *Saeculi noni auctoris in Boetii "Consolationem Philosophiae" commentarius,* Papers and Monographs of the American Academy in Rome 9 (Rome, 1935).
21. The full text is in Appendix I.

Enraged, Juno descended to earth, beat the girl severely, and transformed her into a bear. But Arcas grew into a young hunter who one day happened upon his mother the bear and, in his ignorance, attacked her. Even Jupiter found this unseemly and so made constellations of them both. Her anger increased by this new honor, Juno pleaded with the gods of the sea not to suffer "la putain" and her son to dip into the ocean. And that is why these constellations do not set like the others.

What makes this example so astonishing to us is the context into which it is set, for meter 6 of Book IV is a profound lyric expression of the theme of the common bond of mutual love by which all things seek to hold to the supreme good:

> Sic aeternos reficit cursus
> Alternus amor, sic astrigeris
> Bellum discors exulat oris.

In this elevated context of universal love, with its specific references to the absence of discord in the heavens, this little fable might unintentionally take on a wryly undercutting function, and its downright talk of seduction, pregnancy, assault and battery, whores, and divine vengeance might grate harshly against the smooth Boethian harmonies if we did not know that such inorganic juxtapositions are exactly characteristic of much quite unironic medieval art. More will be said of this later. Here it will simply be observed that one effect of such juxtapositions is to return the *Consolatio* some distance along the road to satire as it was anciently understood by those authors cited earlier who allowed cynicism and obscenity to mingle with higher things in their medleys of prose and verse. While the value of the effects here is dubious, as it has been largely throughout this initial chapter, it will not remain so in the examples to come. In them will be demonstrated, I hope, the great extent to which these narrative interpolations medievalize in positive ways of lasting value the themes of Boethius's evergreen consolation.

II

King on a Wheel

<blockquote>The Historian in his bare was hath many times that which we call fortune to overrule the best wisdom. Many times he must tell events whereof he can yield no cause: or, if he do, it must be poetically.</blockquote>

Sidney, Defense of Poesy

THE MEDIEVAL FRENCH TRANSLATORS of Boethius regularly elaborated, occasionally at great length, the historical citations scattered throughout the *Consolatio*. Preliminary to any discussion of what they did with these notices, however, it is necessary to draw a distinction between Boethius's use of history as incidental fact and history as exemplary illustration. Normally, such glosses as the translators supply to merely factual notices are brief and informative, such as Jean de Meun's gloss on Theodoric's *coemption,* which, by scribal elaboration, became 150 words in Chaucer's final version.

In the course of outlining his personally costly services to the state in Book I, prose 4:44–9, Boethius mentions his efforts to unfix food prices during a famine: "Cum acerbae famis tempore grauis atque inexplicabilis indicta coemptio profligatura inopia Campaniam prouinciam uideretur, certamen aduersum praefectum praetorii communis commodi ratione suscepi, rege cognoscente contendi et ne coemptio exigeretur, euici." The MSS of Jean de Meun's translation and Chaucer's version exhibit successive expansions of this original text and its associated glosses. Part of the reason for the expansion is the common feeling that the reader needs more information, but equally important for our understanding of how medieval texts grow is the fact that Jean carried the odd word *coemptio* directly into his version. The most primitive state of his text reads:

Comme coemption, c'est a dire communs achéz griéz et non mie desploiables, commandéz et establiz seur le peuple ou temps de la fain

33

eigre fust veüz a degaster et a tormenter par souffrete et par mesaise champaigne et province, je reçui l'estrif encontre le provost de pretoire par la raison du commun profit. Je, le roi cognoissant, estrivé et vainqui que la coempcion ne fust requise ne ne passast. [Dedeck-Héry, ed., pp. 177–78]

Only a short time after this first state appeared, a long gloss was added after the word *comme*: "le roi Theodoric qui par un chier temps avoit ses greniers plains de bles commanda que cist blé fust chierement vendu et fist crier ban que nus n'achetast blé fors que le sien jusques a tant qu'il eust tout vendu, je Boece alai contre cest establissement et le vainqui, le roi meïsmes sachant et cognoissant." This is in part a gloss and in part another translation of the last lines of the original Latin paragraph. Still later, two MSS revise the gloss on *coemption,* giving after *peuple*: "Comme au temps de l'aigre fain fust establie ou criee grieve et male a espondre coemption, la quele si comme l'en vëoit bien devoit trop domagier et tormenter la province de Champagne, je pris l'estrif encontre le prevost du pretoire et le roy sachant, je estrivoi."

The effect of this new reading is to correct and refine the language of the preceding version. For example, it corrects the reading of *Campaniam prouinciam* and replaces the overstrong *degaster* with the more general *domagier.* Using this text of Jean's version, Chaucer added a bit of information derived from the following gloss by Nicholas Trevet: "Quicumque modium frumenti emeret, daret regi quintam partem." Chaucer's version, swollen by all of these currents, reads:

Glosa. Whan that Theodoric, the kyng of Gothes, in a dere yeer, hadde his garneeris ful of corn, and comaundede that no man schulde byen no coorn till his corn were soold, and that at a grevous dere prys, Boece withstood that ordenaunce and overcom it, knowynge al this the kyng himselve. Textus. Whan it was in the sowre hungry tyme, ther was establissed or cryed grevous an unplitable coempcioun, that men seyen wel it shulde gretly tormenten and endamagen al the provynce of Campayne, I took stryf ayens the provost of the pretorie for commune profit; and, the kyng knowynge of it, Y overcom it, so that the coempcioun ne was nat axid ne took effect. Coempcioun is to seyn comune achat or beyinge togidre, that were establissed upon the people by swich a manere imposicioun, as whoso boughte a busschel corn, he most yyve the kynge the fyfte part. [Robinson, ed., p. 324]

Thirty Latin words have been drawn into 150 words in the vernacular, and many medieval hands have helped in the pulling. Incidentally, the glossator of the revised mixed version brought it all up to date by comparing it with the famous *gabelle* on salt established in 1341.

It was to this sort of gloss that Jean de Meun and his revisors limited themselves in their rare excursions beyond the Boethian letter. But even this variety of annotation can produce arresting effects, as does the gloss in the revised mixed version which cites some modern instances of worthies whom death has confronted violently: "Note ci des nouveaux exemples de la cheitiveté ou misere des roys de nostre temps, comme du roy Edouart d'Angleterre, qui fu mort par les siens; item du roy Andry . . . en nostre temps La Broce, Marrigny, Guillaume Guette, Pierre Remy, Jordain de Lille, Henri Capel, Olivier de Clicon, Le comte d'Eu, connestable de France"[1] —all of whom were killed around the second quarter of the four-teenth century.

By far the most impressive example of this sort of background history appears in the lengthy prologue of the Anonymous of Meun in which he devotes over 500 lines to recreating the sixth-century milieu in which Boethius was condemned to death. Resorting to chapter 11, Book 17, of Vincent of Beauvais's *Speculum historiale,* the Anonymous gleaned details about the *Gotyens* and their land beyond the *Danubes* and the Roman emperor *Valent*'s struggles with the *Wisegos* and the *Estregos.* Woven also into this account are notices of the realms of *Espaigne, Galice, Aufrique,* and *Lombardie,* and the personalities of *Theodorique, Oudonacre, Pape Jehans,* and Boethius's father-in-law, *Synacus.* In all, it is a noteworthy account to have appeared in a vernacular tongue.

Of greater moment for the present discussion, however, are those historical examples which Boethius himself cites as relevant to the illustration of his philosophical message. In these, the translators found available for their elucidations such figures as the tyrant Dionysius the Elder, Romulus, Regulus, Fabricius, Brutus, Cato, Nero, Seneca, and others to whom Boethius alluded, sometimes obliquely, as he conjured up instances which gave structure and perspective to the terror of his own situation.

While the translators' glosses include such curious legends as that of Zeno's biting the ear of Phalaris, for the purposes of a discussion of the ways in which medieval authors reinterpreted Boethian ideas, the story of

---

1. MS Nat. Lib. of Wales 5039, fols. 33 and 33v. Edward II died in 1327; Andrew of Hungary was strangled in 1345; Gerard Guette, Chancellor of Philippe le Long, died in the reign of Charles le Bel; the Count of Eu in 1350. See Paulin Paris, *Les MSS françois de la Bibliothèque du Roi,* 5 (Paris, 1852):41–2.

Croesus, king of Lydia (ca. 560–546) is the most useful. It is so partly because almost all of the translators—as well as Jean de Meun, Boccaccio, and Chaucer—essayed it. The reasons for its popularity are easy to see. Boethius's Latin account is brief: "Nesciebas Croesum regem Lydorum Cyro paulo ante formidabilem mox deinde miserandum rogi flammis traditum misso caelitus imbre defensum?" (Book II, prose 2:34–6). But it is extremely important, because it is bracketed with explicit statements about the operation of Fortune and the nature of tragedy. Indeed, it is probably because of the association of this definition of tragedy with the story of Croesus, that Chaucer used both story and definition to conclude his *Monk's Tale* of fallen notables.

In the statements immediately preceding the example of Croesus, Philosophy speaks in the persona of Fortune and justifies her ways to man. Of interest are both the pattern and motive of her actions. The pattern is simple polarity, and the motive is conformity with the lawful operation of non-human nature: "*Licet* anno terrae uultum nunc floribus frugibusque redimire, nunc nimbis frigoribusque confundere. *Ius* est mari nunc ..." (23–5). The morphological parallelism of *frugibusque* with *frigoribusque* emphasizes the polarity and rightness of the seasons as frost follows upon fruit. And so Fortune deals with man, with an added touch of pleasure in the process: "Haec nostra uis est, hunc continuum ludum ludimus; rotam uolubili orbe uersamus, infima summis summa infimis mutare gaudemus" (28–31). Here again the syntactical symmetry recalls the simple inverse relation of the two states—weal and woe—of human fortune and the irrelevance of human qualities of will and intention to these sublunary processes.

Tragedy consists in the outcry against this situation. Following the Croesus example, Fortune asks: "Quid tragoediarum clamor aliud deflet nisi indiscreto ictu fortunam felicia regna uertentem?" (38–40). The implication here is that Fortune is so indiscriminate that she will regularly and mechanically throw down the happy and, it is important to add, the guiltless. For Boethius it is tragic to expect any other treatment, and humans are free at least to control their expectations. But for some medieval authors, as we shall see, it is tragic to have deserved such treatment. When Chaucer translated this passage for the conclusion of the *Monk's Tale*, he made a significant change by characterizing the victims as "regnes that ben prowde." Between this simple textual alteration and a great Boethian tragedy like *Troilus and Criseyde* lies the bulk of variations played upon the pattern and motive of Fortune's actions and their tragic consequences to be found in the medieval translations of the *Consolatio*. But before we begin to discriminate among these accounts it will be of use to have as a touchstone a fuller and more authoritative narration of the story of Croesus than Boethius supplies.

Herodotus divides the major portion of his first Book between accounts of the careers of Croesus and Cyrus. Two aspects of his treatment are of interest here. While no very clear picture emerges of a central force behind Croesus's downfall, that fall has been considerably managed in a literary way to provide a rich historical narrative. Herodotus locates the ultimate cause of Croesus's suffering neither in his own character nor, as Boethius does, in a dispassionate, non-rational principle of change. But neither does he let the facts fall where they may.

The main details that characterize his treatment of the story are these. Croesus is seen early demanding of Solon, the wise man of Athens, some recognition of his particularly blest estate (1.29–33) and getting only the reply that no one can be judged fortunate until he is dead.[2] We see his first reversal in the fates of his sons: one is born deaf and dumb; the other, Atys, is inadvertently slain by Adrastus. Croesus's interpretation of the oracles leads him to befriend the Spartans and undertake a war with Cyrus, which he loses. Two important scenes follow. The first is his deliverance from the pyre—the event central to all accounts from Boethius's aside to the twenty-five stanzas in John Lydgate's *Fall of Princes*. And the second is his confrontation of the Delphic oracle. In this latter scene, Croesus chides the priestess for having let the gods deceive him by implying that he could attack the Persians successfully. In the priestess's withering reply we can discern some of the forces that entrapped Croesus: a relentless determinism stemming from an offence some five generations back, the favorable but insufficient intervention of the gods in delaying the fall of Sardis and rescuing Croesus from the pyre, and, finally, in his failure to probe the original oracle, Croesus's recognition of his own *hamartia*. In the self-recognition of this flaw, of course, we can see one of the links that Herodotus makes between history and tragedy.

The scene at the pyre is important because of its centrality to the medieval accounts of Croesus. These, however, differ markedly from that

---

2. Herodotus, ed. and trans. A. D. Godley, rev. ed. Loeb Classical Library (London, 1926), vol. 1.

of Herodotus (1.86), who relates that Cyrus sent Croesus to the flames because, having heard that he was a god-fearing man, Cyrus wanted to see whether any god would save him. It then develops that Cyrus and his interpreters, on listening to Croesus reminisce about Solon, repent of the decision to burn him and order the fire quenched. When Cyrus's servants cannot do so, Croesus cries to Apollo and is rewarded with a shower that not only extinguishes the blaze but persuades Cyrus that Croesus is "a good man and one beloved of the gods." Such remarks, coupled with Herodotus's observations about the many pious offerings made by Croesus around Greece, and the humanizing details about his unfortunate sons, serve to obscure further the roles played in his downfall by the gods and his own guilt.

In spite of this uncertainty about the major force driving Croesus down, it is clear that Herodotus contrived a literary narrative about the process that has discernible tragic overtones. He achieved these by a variety of means, two of which call for notice here. First, Herodotus enforces the inevitability of Croesus's fall by making repeated glances forward to it in digressions. This constant foreshadowing contributes a solid sense of inevitability to the history that undercuts the equivocation of the explicit interpretations. The second literary strategy, and the one which at least one French translator rediscovered, is the establishment of symmetry between the careers of Croesus and Cyrus. This is achieved on a variety of levels: for example, the parallels to be seen in both kings' misinterpretations of oracles, dreams, and portents. The relation between the two kings that is of chief significance, however, is Cyrus's acceptance of the counsel of Croesus, now his slave, to attack the Massagetae, a decision that leads to Cyrus's death in defeat. In the speech in which he gives this counsel, his last in the book, Croesus unwittingly—and Herodotus intentionally—engages in irony and, furthermore, employs what came to be in the Middle Ages the chief emblem of tragedy:

> "Sire," said he, "you have ere how heard from me that since Zeus has given me to you I will to the best of my power turn aside whatever mischance I see threatening your house. And disaster has been my teacher. Now if you deem yourself and the army that you lead to be immortal, it is not for me to give you advice; but if you know that you and those whom you rule are but men, then I must first teach you this: men's fortunes are on a wheel (*kuklos*), which in its turning suffers not the same man to prosper forever. Then, if that be true, I am

not of that same mind on the business in hand as these your other counsellors."[3]

With such heavily dramatic devices at work in his narration, Herodotus could afford to be somewhat vague in his strictly historical explanations of the fates of Croesus and Cyrus. He had tragedy working for his history, and, in their own ways, so did the medieval translators of Boethius.

The translators' glosses and adaptations of the story of Croesus range from the 150-word and 200-word accounts in the earliest prose version and the revised mixed version, through the 75 lines of Renaut de Louhans's verse, to the 240 lines composed by the Anonymous of Meun. Such a succession of variations on a theme allows us to explore the changes rung by medieval authors on the relation of a personified Fortune to individual men's fates. In the hope of demonstrating how the interpolated narratives put the medieval stamp on the Boethian conceptions of Fortune and tragedy, I shall also appeal to treatments of the story of Croesus in other vernacular works contemporary with the French translations.

All of the translators render Boethius's explicit statements on Fortune and tragedy that bracket the example of Croesus, and, indeed, there is some interesting matter in their treatments. Renaut de Louhans, for example, extends the genre of tragedy to encompass some familiar medieval works:

> Regarde bien la tragedie
> Quant l'on fait une bonne feste
> Que menestriers chantent de geste
> Soit de Rolent et d'Olivier,
> Soit de Charloy ou soit d'Ogier.[4]

But it is in their narration of the story of Croesus itself that the translators, now transformed into adaptors, reveal most accurately the actual positions of their concepts of Fortune, history, and tragedy around the Boethian nucleus. There were many possibilities. In his sketch of the medieval setting of Chaucer's *Monk's Tale*,[5] R. W. Babcock sorted the documents into three "traditions." The Roman, leading from Ovid and Hyginus to Boccaccio by way of Boethius and Isidore of Seville, develops

3. Herodotus, 1.261.
4. MS B. N. fr. 578, fol. 15.
5. R. W. Babcock, "The Medieval Setting of Chaucer's *Monk's Tale*," *PMLA* 46 (1931):205–13.

the theme of fickle Fortune. The Clerical, comprising the moralistic exploitation of "falls" by such authors as Hugh of St. Victor, Innocent III, Jacques de Vitry, and John of Bromyard, extended after Chaucer into the works of Laurent de Premierfait and John Lydgate. And finally, the non-Clerical, or narrative, tradition which includes Simon de Freine's *Roman de Philosophie,* the *Speculum Stultorum,* and the *Roman de la Rose* is the tradition that, along with the Roman, stands behind Chaucer. Rather than relate the translators' various versions of Croesus to such traditions, I think it is aesthetically more illuminating to probe the ways in which those translators who were interested in what we would call narrative structure and irony exploited the possibilities inherent in the notion of tragedy, while those more inclined toward characterization and psychology played with Fortuna.

The gloss appended to the earliest French translation of the *Consolatio* is derived, like most of the expansions on mythological themes in that work, not, as Pierre Courcelle implies, from the commentary of William of Conches, but from the Vatican Mythographies.[6] In this gloss we can see in germ one direction medieval authors would take in interpreting the story of Croesus: "Cirus prist Cresum, e por ce que il l'aveit molt grevé s'il comanda aardeir, il eschapa, defenduz par une grant pluie, e recovra son honor. Aprés se gloirefieit de sa beneurance. Salon, li uns de set sages d'Athenes, dist a lui, 'Nul home se deit glorefier en cest siecle, com il ne sache quel chose li jors de demain apareille a lui'."[7] The gloss goes on to relate the interpretation given to a dream of Croesus's by his daughter, Phania, a creature invented by the ninth-century commentator Remigius of Auxerre.[8] Two things are notable in the gloss. First, it implies that Croesus's self-glorification is connected with his fall. After Solon's speech, Croesus as a person disappears, perhaps because his pride cost him his humanity. Things simply happen to his body: "Il sereit pris de rechef del cel meesmes enemi, e sereit levez en croiz. E Jupiter l'oindreit, ce est la pluie le moillereit, e li soleil le sechereit, e en tel manier avint." The second

---

6. Pierre Courcelle, "Étude critique sur les commentaires de la Consolation de Boèce (IXe–XVe siècles)," *Archives d'histoire doctrinale et littéraire du moyen âge* 14 (1939):95; Georg H. Bode, *Scriptores rerum mythicarum latini tres* (Cellis, 1834), pp. 59–60 and 137.
7. MS Vienna 2642, fol. 11v.
8. H. F. Stewart, "A Commentary by Remigius Autissiodorensis on the *De Cons. Phil.* of Boethius," *Journal of Theological Studies* 17 (1915–16):42.

thing to note is the beginnings of a dramatic treatment of the tale in the direct address given to Solon.

The interpretation of this legend by William of Conches as it appears in the gloss added to the revised mixed version is more complex than that derived from the Vatican Mythographies and suggests a contest between God and the Devil within the person of Croesus. The king is deceived by Apollo and rescued by "the Divine Will," but both allow him to exercise to the full his capacity for human frailty. Croesus's fatal sin of pride is explicit.

> Cestui Cressus, quant il se devoit combatre contre Cyrus, requist au dieu Apolin savoir qu'il lui avendroit, si lui respondit par amphibolie doublement comme fait le Dÿable ainsi, "Cressus perdet alim transgressus maxima regna." Si entendi en une maniere qu'il descomvoit le royaume Cyrus, et il n'avint pas ainsi, mais fut vaincu par Cyrus. Si fut prins et mené au feu pour ardoir et puis fut delivré par la volunté divine. Si avint qu'il s'en commença a glorifier et enorgueillir.[9]

One MS of the revised mixed version—B. M. Harley 4330—notes (fol. 30) that the example of Croesus appears in the *Roman de la Rose,* and it is worth turning to Jean de Meun's account not only because it appears in time between the interpretations of William of Conches and Renaut de Louhans but also because it is a useful illustration of the qualifications that actual narrative usages place on the abstract statements of scholastics. Whereas lines 4837–4974 of the *Roman* give a substantially Boethian view of the work of Fortune, being in fact a near-translation of the *Consolatio*'s Book II, prose 8, Jean de Meun's version of the story of Croesus is complicated and modified by the overriding themes and methods of the *Roman de la Rose.*

In the course of her lengthy interpretation of the puzzling dream of Croesus, Phania paints a Boethian miniature of Fortuna:

> Si destruit ele maint preudome,
> Qu'el ne prise pas une pome
> Tricherie ne leiauté,
> Ne vil estat, ne reiauté;
> Anceis s'en jeue a la pelote,
> Come pucele nice e sote,
> E giete a grant desordenance
> Richece, eneur e reverence.[10]

9. MS Nat. Lib. of Wales 5039, fol. 18v.
10. *Le Roman de la Rose,* ed. Ernest Langlois, Société des anciens textes français, 5 vols. (Paris, 1914–24), vol. 3, lines 6553–60.

Two things contort the motions of this witless tennis player, however, and they are the love theme of the *Roman* and the psychologizing methods of its authors. The latter part of Phania's address to her hapless father consists of her praise for *Gentillece,* personified as the daughter of Fortune and the only being for whom the goddess cares. Now, it is possible that true gentility, stoutly maintained, might produce an insouciance toward Fortune's gifts somewhat analogous to Boethian stoicism, but the picture of so fated a man as Croesus, to whom the gods have vouchsafed visions of his doom, absorbing instruction on fine manners from a winsome girl is absurd. *Gentilece* is, of course, a wholly necessary aspect of Jean's theme of love, as much as procreation, which frustrates the universal prospect of death. But news of the power of courtesy, as Jean knows, arrives too late for Croesus.

Also in league against a dogmatic use of Fortune as an instrument to explain men's fates is the artful psychology of the dramatic contest between Phania and her father over their rival interpretations of his dream:

> "Fille," fait il, "de courtesie
> Ne de sen ne m'aprencz mie;
> Plus en sai que vous ne savez,
> Qui si chastié m'en avez.
> E quant par vostre fol respons
> M'avez mon songe ainsinc espons,
> Servi m'avez de granz mençonges;
> Car sachiez que cist nobles songes,
> Ou fausse glose voulez metre,
> Deit estre entenduz a la letre;
> E je meïsmes l'i entens,
> Si con nous le verrons en tens.
> Onc ausinc noble vision
> N'ot si vil esposicion.
> Le deu, sachiez, a mei vendront,
> E le servise me rendront
> Qu'il m'ont par cet songe tramis,
> Tant est chascuns d'aus mes amis,
> Car bien l'ai pieça deservi."

[lines 6601–19]

Thus Croesus is finely realized as a prideful pedant and his daughter as a devotee of *fin amour,* but these satirical portraits, filled as they are with humanizing detail, leave little room for the simple mechanical motions of Fortune's old wheel, or even her new racquet. Both symbols are too crude for their jobs.

The interpretation of the story of Croesus given by the Dominican friar Renaut de Louhans is significantly different from the others considered in this chapter because of its clear insistence on the direct role of the prosopopoeia of Fortune in men's affairs and because of its clever exploitation of a serious misreading of the Latin text. From the very first word of his account, Renaut emphasizes the posturing presence of Dame Fortune—"Je croy bien," she says, summoning our attention to Croesus's high estate before his humiliating fall, his never-empty purse, his riches and his valor. The possibility of stressing Fortune's personal role had always been there, because Philosophy narrates this entire passage in her persona, but Renaut is the only writer to make her so insistently present in the episode. We see this as she points to her repeated interventions in Croesus's life, without always giving her reasons for them. At first she simply says, "I completely changed my manner," when the once-great Croesus was captured by the king of Persia. She is silent also on who sent the life-saving rain, which just came. But after Croesus, who ought to have been humble, began to strut and raised himself by vainglory and failed to think on her, she exclaims, "Fis je la moe / Car aprés je tournay ma roe."

At this point Renaut brings in the portentous dream and its interpretation by the unnamed daughter of Croesus, whom Renaut takes some care to characterize. She is frightened, appropriately, both by her father and by the contents of his vision, and she in no way resembles the sententious love-struck girl depicted by Jean de Meun:

> Quant elle ouÿ la vision
> Si fut en grant affliction,
> Car vit la fin que fut amere,
> Si ne l'ose dire a son pere
> Tant que son pere l'en blasma.
> Lors en ceste guise parla,
> "Pere, voulez vous que je die
> Ce que vo songe signifie?"[11]

And so it came to pass that in a little while the king of Persia seized him and hanged him from a gibbet. So much for Croesus, but for Renaut the story is not over. Not for nothing is Cyrus never named in this account, for Renaut seems to have assumed that the king of Persia who destroyed Croesus was the same King Perses whom Boethius mentions in a line following his notice of Croesus and before his remarks on tragedy:

11. MS B. N. fr. 578, fols. 14v–15.

"Num te praeterit Paulum Persi regis a se capti calamitatibus pias inpendisse lacrimas?" (Book II, prose 2:36–8). By connecting the tragedy of this King Perses with that of Croesus—they were in fact separated in history by some 380 years—Renaut creates a symmetry and poetic justice in the acts of Fortune that remind us of the perfect Judge behind her, directing her choices if not her fickle manner.

The effect of Renaut's innovation is clear. The continuous presence of the humanized Fortuna, who manipulates the guilty Croesus like a puppet, makes less mechanical the action of the Boethian personification. And, even though Croesus does not make proper use of his free will, the existence of a human will free to contemn the world is manifested here in the untemptable stoic Paulus, who cared nothing for palaces and treasures and the other gifts of Fortune and consequently defeated King Perses and wept for him too.

Finally, to round off this discussion of Renaut with a glance back at Jean de Meun, we may note that one manuscript of Renaut's version of the *Consolatio* also contains a copy of the *Roman de la Rose* written by the same scribe (MS B. N. fr. 812), and that that scribe added to Renaut's version a passage inspired by Jean's account of Croesus. Following the line "Que Jupiter vous moullera," this scribe wrote:

> "Beau pere," ce dit Phanie,
> Sa fille qui moult fu corrucie,
> "Se votre vie n'amendez,
> Par autre serez amendez."
> Ce dit Cressus, "Ja n'avendra,
> Ne ja mon cueur ne le croira
> Que si tres noble vision
> Ait si malle exposicion."

[fol. 14v]

This angry, pithy girl is just the sort of hybrid that the manuscript process of compilation engenders, bearing the likeness of neither of the answerable parents.

In the first chapter I characterized the Dominican Renaut and the Anonymous of Meun as classicizers of the kind recognized by Beryl Smalley as existing among the English friars. And the Anonymous may himself have been a member of the preaching order. Where Renaut made extensive use of the classicizing commentaries of his fellow Dominican Nicholas Trevet, the Anonymous employed as fully the works of another

Dominican, Vincent of Beauvais. Although Renaut and the Anonymous made vernacular verse translations of a secular work and not Latin prose commentaries on sacred ones, they do share with Smalley's English academic mendicants an undisguised and often enthusiastic interest in the literature, history, and mythology of classical antiquity for their own sake.[12] This interest is amply demonstrated in the Anonymous's treatment of the story of Croesus, which at the same time exhibits his ability to shape Vincent's encyclopedic details into the sort of tragedy that would easily have found a place among the hundred in the cell of Chaucer's Monk and, oddly enough, might also have drawn the approval of his Knight for a reason which we shall see.

But first his flaws. The thoroughness of the Anonymous's scholarship makes him something of a slave to circumstantial detail. Thus, when he comes upon Vincent's description of the rivers crossed by Cyrus, he cannot resist culling details about the dimensions—breadths and depths—of the streams, and citing second-hand Vincent's authorities: Martianus, Lucan, and Solinus.[13] He goes on to mention the eels which in those streams reach a prodigious size—which he gives, "around thirty feet in length," and so on and on. Such details, of course, soon exhaust their value in establishing verisimilitude.

When we turn to the account of Croesus proper, we see at once both how concerned the Anonymous is with our grasping the lesson of the exemplum and the fact that he perceives a real structure in the narrative:

> Et pour Fortune miex entendre
> Voel mon parler plus loing estendre
> De ces .ii. roys qui jadis furent
> Qui par long temps contens eürent.[14]

The long contest between the two sovereigns is to be his subject then, but first he devotes some 150 lines to describing Cyrus's conquest of Babylon—with a digression on its dimensions. It is only after the Anonymous begins to narrate Belshazzar's feast that we see the parallel being drawn between Daniel's interpreting the ominous handwriting on the wall for the impious Balthasar and the many later portents that Croesus ignores at his

12. Beryl Smalley, *English Friars and Antiquity in the Early Fourteenth Century* (Oxford, 1960), p. 7.
13. Vincent of Beauvais, *Speculum historiale* 4, 11. I have used MS B. N. lat. 4897.
14. MS B. N. fr. 576, fol. 19.

peril. No sooner has Daniel expounded the third word than Cyrus puts the guests to flight. But the miraculous speech that springs to the lips of Croesus's once-dumb son, Athis, restrains Cyrus from vengeance:

> "Cyrus, Fortune tresmuee,
> Com tu vois, et mi et mon pere
> De prosperité en misere,
> T'argüe pour nous et te somme,
> Que tu te congnoisces pour homme
> A qui il poët mesavenir,
> Si com tu nous vois avenir.
> Dont raisons te doit esmouvoir
> A pitet de nos mauls avoir."

[fol. 20]

Having ignored the example of his friend Balthasar who failed to heed a miraculous warning, Croesus now disregards the very marvel that moved the relentless Cyrus to his only merciful act. Not only is Croesus pictured here as unfeeling, he is also subsequently shown in the guise of a political rebel:

> Mais aprés celle grace belle
> Fist Cresus traïson nouvelle
> Contre Cyrus, et esmut guerre
> Pour fouler son regne et sa terre.

[fol. 20]

The opaque and implacable Cyrus seizes him again, and once more Fortune spares him, this time from the pyre. Thus having been delivered for the third time by a clearly providential intervention, Croesus, though unpsychologized and seen only from the outside, is now clearly labelled a bad one ("li malvais Cresus") and hardly worth the last great effort that God himself, according to Phania, expends in trying to alert him to the inevitable plunge that must follow so many unmerited deliverances:

> "Biaus peres, pechiés que t'enpence
> D'orguel et d'outrecuiderie
> Te doit briefment tollir la vie,
> Pour ce que tu n'as remembrance
> Jadis de ta double mescance;
> Comment Cyrus t'a desconfit,
> Et des graces que Diex te fit
> Sauver ta vie et le tien rendre.
> Et si voels de nouvel emprendre

> Contre Cyrus et rebeller,
> Dont Diex t'a volut reveler
> L'issue qui t'en avenra."

[fol. 20v]

From these excerpts I think it can be seen that the Anonymous has hit, however amateurishly, upon one of the richest resources of Boethian tragedy, namely, the revelation through structure, through cumulative repetitions, of the terrible swings of weal and woe to which human life is subject, regardless of personal merit. The Croesus of the Anonymous of Meun starts out more blind than evil, and his inability to spell out the meaning of repeated signs is reminiscent of the hapless Palamon and Arcite of the *Knight's Tale* who are introduced barely breathing in a heap of corpses and whose subsequent lives go "Now up, now doun, as boket in a welle."

The translation of the *Consolatio* printed by Colard Mansion in 1477 simply represents Croesus as a lucky man: "Mais tantost aprés il, miserable, pris par le dict Cyrus, appliqué aux flambes embrasées, fut defendu de Fortune, luy favorisant par une pluie envoyée du ciel."[15] The account is useful, however, for it reminds us that the story is told by "Jehan Bocace en son livre du *Dechiet des nobles hommes.*" And it is worth turning to a vernacular version of that work for a final contrast with the medieval portrait by the Anonymous of Meun. Boccaccio's *De Casibus* was translated into French by Laurent de Premierfait and from this version into English by John Lydgate.[16] In this latter state we can see a medley of details from the encyclopedic tradition on which the Anonymous of Meun drew.

Lydgate begins his Book II with assurances that it is not Fortune who gives men the fall but vicious living, and that Fortune has no dominion over princes governed by reason. But as he relates successively the stories of Balthasar and Daniel, the "accidental" slaying of Croesus's son, the defeat of Balthasar and Croesus by Cyrus—with the anecdote of the providential rain—and, finally, the slaughter of Cyrus and his army by Queen Tomyris, it becomes apparent that the role of Croesus is reduced to that of an innocent and uncomprehending victim of the tyrant Cyrus, who is the one ultimately to suffer divine retribution. In Croesus's initial prosperity,

15. Quoted from the reprinting by Antoine Verard (Paris, 1494), fol. 43.
16. See *Lydgate's Fall of Princes,* ed. Henry Bergen, Early English Text Society, extra series 121–4, 4 vols. (London, 1924–7).

"nothyng stood amys," and his son's death is "causeles," whereas, "Cruel Cirus with malice was atteynt," and:

> whan he gan presumptiousli entende
> To robbe and reue folk thoruh his pillage,
> God & Fortune made hym to descende
> Ful sodenli from his roial stage.

[lines 3746–9]

Thus, while Lydgate's treatment of Cyrus is consistent with medieval views on the purposeful nature of suffering, the interpretation of the fate of Croesus, in structural emphasis similar to that by the Anonymous of Meun, tastes something like its Boethian original. Croesus in no way deserves either his joy or woe, which succeed one another like clockwork: "ther is non so gret a sorwe, / But it must cese, outher eue or morwe." Lydgate also teaches Fortune's lesson through symmetry—here the balance is between the fates of Croesus and Cyrus—but his monkish mind is also fixed on the delicious pathos of Croesus's condition and the thrilling rightness of Cyrus's dismemberment by a woman. Where Boethian man had free will, not to change his fate so much as ignore it, Lydgate's pathetic Croesus is not only helpless but also too innocent, an ironic hero whose suffering is merely interesting.

Neither Jean de Meun nor Renaut shows much interest in making tragedy of Croesus's situation, but they do adopt Fortune. Both seem to accept that aspect of the newer medieval tradition, sketched by John L. Grigsby,[17] that makes Fortune the bailiff of God, the judge who probes our culpability. Jean and, to a lesser extent, Renaut turn their art to characterizing the guilty parties. But both authors also extend their psychologizing to the persona of Fortune and use the notion of play fixed on her (*ludum ludimus*) to humanize and satirize her as a "pucele, nice et sote" or the fickle busybody who cries "En jouer est toute ma joye!" So exclusively are human minds the interest of Jean de Meun's account, and so diminished are plot events, that he never names Cyrus and resorts to impersonal constructions in indicating what actually happens to Croesus: "Puis le mist l'en au col la bride."

In other words, the replacement of Boethius's simple, irrational agency by a medieval one, highly motivated by notions of Justice, has resulted in

---

17. John L. Grigsby, ed., *The Middle French "Liber Fortunae"*, Univ. of California Pubs. in Modern Philology 81 (Berkeley and Los Angeles, 1967), p. 15.

increased attention to human qualities, even in the personifications. The victims are more carefully drawn and the mediating automata more delicately articulated, because it is human psychology that is beginning to rule both earth and heaven.

Lydgate and the Anonymous of Meun, on the other hand, seize on the tragic potential in the structure of the story of Croesus, while merely making the proper noises about Fortune. Although Lydgate had learned his Chaucer well enough to take pathos where he found it, the lack of guilt in his Croesus returns a Boethian tone to the story. Tragedy is the outcry against such unforeseen reversals as Croesus experienced, and tragedy becomes ironic to the extent that the audience can see the reversals coming. It is the contribution of the Anonymous of Meun that he regularized the pendulation of events above the head of Croesus and so raised an exemplum to tragic status. The complementary interests of Renaut and the Anonymous in characterization and underlying structure, psychology and dramatic irony, thus bring to the medieval French versions of the *Consolatio* something of those polarized points of view that see tragedy now as a *process* set in motion by the violation of moral law, human or divine, now as a *condition* mysteriously imposed by an omnipotent external fate.[18]

18. See Northrop Frye, *Anatomy of Criticism* (Princeton, 1957), pp. 209–10.

III

The Tempting Integument

> *Now, wirthy folk, Boece, that senatour,*
> *To wryt this fenyeit fable tuk in cure,*
> *In his gay buke of Consolatioun*
> *ffor our doctrene and gud instructioun;*
> *Quhilk in the self suppoiss it fenyeid be,*
> *And hid under the cloik of poetre.*
> Henryson, *Orpheus and Eurydice,* 415–20

WHEN BOETHIUS had Lady Philosophy contemn the self-serving Stoics and Epicureans for tearing the garment she had woven with her own hands, he used a metaphor that came to be developed in the Middle Ages into a theory of truth in Scripture and, with weaker claims, in fiction. For the philosophic commentators on secular works, such as William of Conches and Nicholas Trevet, borrowed the theologians' notion that God's naked truth is veiled from vulgar eyes in Holy Writ and that it is the task of the theologians to reveal it, and the loan included the tripartite division of scriptural senses into literal, moral, and allegorical.

Medieval terminology for the allegorical sense varied from *integumentum* in William of Conches and John of Garland to *involucrum* in Peter Abelard and John of Salisbury, but its meaning was stable. This is to be seen in the succinct definition given by Bernard Silvester, who used both terms, in his commentary on the *Aeneid*: "Integumentum vero est genus demonstrationis sub fabulosa narratione veritatis involvens intellectum, unde et involucrum dicitur."[1] The terminology was also somewhat accessible to the laity through such works as the *Roman de la Rose*, where it is

---

1. This quotation and the basis for my discussion are drawn from Édouard Jeauneau, "L'Usage de la notion d'integumentum à travers les gloses de Guillaume de Conches," *Archives d'histoire doctrinale et littèraire du moyen âge* 24 (1957): 35–70. See also, M. D. Chenu, "Involucrum: le mythe selon les théologiens médiévaux," *Archives d'hist. Doct. et litt. du moyen âge* 22 (1955):75–9;

51

used by Dame Raison to defend her talk about testicles against the Lover's charge of obscenity—an application of some importance if we are not to misunderstand the frequent appearance of bawdiness in the translations of Boethius. Jean wrote:

> En ma parole autre sen ot,
> Au miens quant de coilles palaie,
> Don si briement paler voulaie,
> Que celui que tu i veauz metre;
> E qui bien entendrait la letre,
> Le sen verrait en l'escriture
> Qui esclarcist la fable ocure;
> La verité dedenz reposte
> Sereit clere s'ele iert esposte;
> Bien l'entendras se bien repetes
> Les *integumenz* aus poetes:
> La verras une grant partie
> Des secrez de philosophie.

[lines 7158–70]

Among the models on which the translators drew for their narrative dilations of the Boethian text, these Latin commentaries of William of Conches and others naturally figure prominently. As I shall show, they are important also for giving the translators something of the terminology noted above concerning the allegorical use of such narratives. In Chapter I, one of the commentators' distinctions in the three-way contrast among fable, history, and integument was mentioned. Here I will explore in more detail the use the translators made of this third term both in theory and practice.

Édouard Jeauneau, on whose discussion my brief notice is based, makes two basic points, both of which need to be qualified in their application to the medieval French translators of the *Consolatio*. The first is that the main technique used by the commentators to reveal the truth beneath the veil of myth was *etymology*; the second point is that they also strove for *polyvalence*.

The etymology found in the commentators was not scientific etymology, of course, but a sort of exercise in ahistorical philological subtlety by

---

Beryl Smalley, *The Study of the Bible in the Middle Ages* (Oxford, 1952); and two fundamental studies: Henri de Lubac, *Exégèse médiévale* (Paris, 1959–64); and Ceslaus Spicq, *Esquisse d'une histoire de l'éxègese latine au moyen âge,* Bibliothèque thomiste 26 (Paris, 1944).

which the essence of a word or proper name was discovered. Their followers, the translators, also made some use of this technique, even when they did not take it directly from the commentaries. But their use of it is limited and subservient to other techniques. On the subject of Boethius's Epicureans and Stoics, for example, Pierre de Paris wrote that the first, "sont dis Epyguriens auci come homes demenans vie de pors, car *epy* en grezois vuet dire *dessous* en franceis, et *guyros* vuet dire *porc.*" The second, "sont apellé Stoyens de cest nom *stoos,* quar *stoos* en gregois vuet dire *fosse* en franceis, dont stoyen vuet dire auci come home habitant en fosses."[2] Appalled by the linguistic ignorance displayed in such etymologizing, Antoine Thomas throws up his hands; it is useless to insist, he says. But it may be urged that in doing so he has failed to recognize the method in the madness of the translator. Pierre may have had small Greek, but the context of Philosophy's complaint clearly indicated that these Epicureans and Stoics were bad people. Pierre therefore finds the essence of the first in their piggishness and of the second in their isolation from others—men who live in pits. Could Plato have asked for more?

For an example of what less inept translators did with the techniques of the professional commentators, I turn first to the lengthy telling of the story of Orpheus by the anonymous Burgundian author of the earliest French translation and its moralization adapted from the commentary of William of Conches. And I will confine my illustrations here to the relations on Orpheus, although I could as easily have used Hercules, to whose labors the Anonymous of Meun and Renaut de Louhans each devote over 300 lines. In the Burgundian's narration on Orpheus we can see not only to what small use the translator put etymology, but also what has become of Jeauneau's second technique of *polyvalence.* By this term, Jeauneau means the valued multiplicity of competing and even contradictory interpretations to which any particular text could give rise. William, for instance, saw Eurydice's descent into hell as a sinful fall, whereas Orpheus's ostensibly similar journey, being made in the spirit of detached observation, symbolized the conversion of the sage from worldly things. This kind of polyvalence was carried into the glosses of the translation printed by Colard Mansion:

2. MS Vat. lat. 4788, fol. 10v. See Antoine Thomas and Mario Roques, "Traductions françaises de la *Cons. Phil.* de Boèce," in *Hist. litt. de la France* (Paris, 1938), 37:445–6.

> Mais a cestuy enfer povons nous descendre par trois voyes. C'est assavoir par nature, par vice, et par vertu. Par nature comme quant l'ame est conjoincte au corps elle, descendant du ciel, descend de sa propre dignité et est subjecte aux passions humaines et corporelles. Par vice comme quant aucun en sacrifiant au dyable parle a eulx, comme il est escript de Eneas, ou comme quant aulcun met toute son intention et voulenté en choses terriennes et vicieuses. Par vertu comme quant aulcun saige descend a la congnoissance des biens temporeux, et comme il n'ayt veü pou ou gueres de [fol. 91] bien en iceulx, tantost il en retrait sa concupiscence illicite. Et par ceste maniere descendirent Hercules et Orpheüs en enfers.

The point I would make about the fate of Jeauneau's polyvalence as it has any relevance to the Burgundian's version and most of the other French translations of the *Consolatio* is that while polyvalence began in William of Conches as an interest in the potential richness of multiple readings of mythic integument, it developed in the translations into a habit of proliferating narrative episodes. William himself is responsible for initiating this habit at least in the telling of the Orpheus legend, for he abandons the strictly Boethian details and adds the late classical story of Aristaeus, which he took from the Vatican Mythographies. In brief, that myth gives the following version of Eurydice's death: one day while wandering through the fields, she met the shepherd Aristaeus who tried to rape her, and in fleeing, she stepped on a serpent whose fatal bite sent her to Hades. William of Conches used this tale to identify Eurydice as Natural Concupiscence or Human Desire. Aristaeus, through the transvaluation beloved by allegorists, becomes Virtue, which seeks to lift Desire from earthly things. Desire flees Virtue and descends to the pleasures of the world.[3]

William's interest in the story was hermeneutic, but the demands it made on narrative content and structure were to be more significant in the translations. As can be seen from the selection in Appendix I, the anony-

---

3. See discussion of William's interpretation in: Charles Jourdain, "Des commentaires inédits de Guillaume de Conches et de Nicholas Triveth sur la Consolation de Boèce," *Notices et extraits de MSS de la Bibliothèque Impériale* 20, 2 (1862):40–82; Jacqueline Hatinguais, "En marge d'un poeme de Boèce: l'interprétation allégorique du mythe d'Orphée par Guillaume de Conches," *Actes du congrès,* Assoc. Guillaume Budé, Congrès de Tours et Poitiers (Paris, 1954), pp. 285–9; John B. Friedman, *Orpheus in the Middle Ages* (Harvard, 1971); and Kenneth R. R. Gros Louis, "Robert Henryson's *Orpheus and Eurydice* and the Orpheus Traditions of the Middle Ages," *Speculum* 41 (1966):643–55.

mous Burgundian found it necessary to retell the story of Orpheus three times: once with its Boethian details; again with the Aristaeus addition and a moralization of details from the first telling; and a third time with a moralization of the Aristaeus matter. One effect of such repeated narrations was to minimize the allegorical interpretation as the translators sought additional narrative details to enliven and distinguish their redactions. An example of this is to be seen in the Burgundian's treatment of William's pairing together the infernal descents of Orpheus and Hercules. The translator turned this into a bit of dialogue as Orpheus protests to the inmates of Hades, "Je ne sui pas ci venuz por batre tun portier come fist Hercules. Je i sui venuz por ma femme, que est morte novelement."

To the narrative texture of the earliest version, the Burgundian also added other medievalizing details. William, for example, had said simply that Tytius's torment was continuous, but the translator added, "Li voltor li manjüent la gole tote la semaine josqu'al samedi, e au lundi est toz entiers." And where William had ended his commentary on Boethius's own solemn note, the Burgundian goes on to warn us about wine and women, for Orpheus was later killed by the priestesses of "Bachi del deu del vin . . . De ce dit Salemons, 'Li vins e les femmes font meesmes les sagese foleer'."

To establish an intermediate stage between the kind of successive retelling sketched above and the form that the narrative was given in the Anonymous of Meun's version, it is useful to observe what the glossator of the revised mixed version did with the glosses from William of Conches a hundred years or so after the earliest translation. To the verse version of the story in its Boethian form, he added a retelling of the whole in some 300 words with an accumulation of details about Aristaeus, the Furies, Pluto, and Rhadamanthus, but at the end he gave only a short moralization of a hundred words—in spite of his protestation that it is unthinkable that so sage a man as Boece would put into his book "sanz cause, fables ne autres choses superfluez." In this version the moralization has become shrunken and inept, but some skill is shown in the relation of such small narrative details as that Eurydice was killed by the serpent's *venom*; that Orpheus's song made the streams run back up hill (contre mont retourner); that the vultures tore Tytius's liver with their *beaks*; and that Tantalus pined for the water at his *chin* and the apple at his *nose*.

The Anonymous of Meun's 1238-line version of the legend of Orpheus is indeed lengthy, twice as long as either the Middle English *Sir Orfeo* or

Robert Henryson's *Orpheus and Eurydice,* but even so it does not deserve the abuse it receives from Antoine Thomas, who finds it verbose, repetitive, and meaninglessly digressive.[4] In order to give the meaning of the Anonymous's version an opportunity to emerge for itself, I will offer a more extensive summary than Thomas's and also indicate the Anonymous's sources.

The Anonymous devotes his first eighty lines to a straightforward translation of the fifty-eight lines of Boethius's meter. He then proposes to show that Boece "a moralité l'a faite / D'amour qui s'est de Dieu retrait." There follow some thirty-eight lines narrating more lyrically the catabasis of Orpheus and the power of love to purge our sins. Twenty lines succeed on Tergeminus—not yet identified as Cerberus—which associate his three heads with the steps to false love: "Plaisance," "Consentir," and "Mailvaise Oevre." Then the Anonymous relates the story of Ixion in some hundred lines, drawing on the *Mithologiae* of Fulgentius with its euhemeristic interpretation of the origin of the centaurs and its moralization of Ixion as the personified desire for dignity:

> Car qui terryene honneur convoite
> Or hault or bas cest roe droite
> Qui lors s'arreste et plus ne tourne
> En coer cui Dieu amours adourne.[5]

[fol. 46v]

Next, Fulgentius is drawn upon for a 105–line narration of the legend of Tantalus, the avaricious man; Pelops, as "fole amour"; and Minerva, who stands for Wisdom. We are told that when Minerva ate the shoulder of Pelops, she diminished his carnal folly, and by replacing it with one of "ivoire cler," she restored him to the pure love of God. The story of Tytius follows, in eighty lines, and for this the Anonymous had to turn elsewhere for information. At first he made up his own details, telling of Tytius and Latona the same story he had just told of Ixion and Juno, but he soon appeals to "the gloss on Boethius" for a moralization that sees Tytius as the "luxureus." This gloss is apparently that of William of Conches, who, like the translator, observes that the tormented liver is the seat of libido.

Next, Orpheus reappears, with some initial comments on music and

4. Thomas and Roques, p. 459.
5. *Fulgentii opera,* ed. R. Helm (Leipzig, 1898), pp. 36–9.

number, again supplied by Fulgentius, in an account of some forty-five lines. And this appearance is followed by a brief and garbled version of the story of Aristaeus, who signifies "Tres bon engien qui subtillie / Erudix de s'amour rouver." The Anonymous thereafter introduces a 125–line discourse on music and mathematics with a Christianizing interpretation that seems to be a mixture of homespun allegories and information taken perhaps from Boethius's *De Musica* or Vincent of Beauvais's *Speculum doctrinale*:

> Li ars de musique est trouvee
> Et non sans plus en creature,
> Mais ou Gouverneur de Nature
> Qui la simplece d'unité
> Multiplie en triplicité
> De la melodie joieuse
> De bonneurté glorïeuse
> Dont unités est li bourdons
> Qui accorde ces .iii. cordons.
> Substance en trois personnes une
> Et est es personnes commune
> En la doulce consonancie
> Qu'ou Saint Espir est alye
> Dou Pere au Fil, du Fil au Pere
> Accors aultres ne si compere.
>
> [fol. 48v]

A long unmoralized account of the story of Arion and the dolphin follows, and this the Anonymous clearly drew from Vincent's *Speculum historiale*.[6] Thereafter, the translator returns to Orpheus, Cerberus, and the Furies for some 145 lines into which is injected much miscellaneous "interpretation" of such things as the triple fountain at which the child Orpheus drank—grammar, logic, rhetoric—and the three heads of Cerberus again, here as Europe, Asia, and Africa.[7] A complex fable ensues (the longest in the account and the one I have chosen for inclusion in Appendix I), for which William of Conches is the source. It begins with a retelling of the Ixion story but quickly passes into a lengthy dramatized narration of the judgment of Paris, in which Juno, Pallas, and the victorious Venus are seen as representative of the active, contemplative, and worldly lives.

6. Vincent of Beauvais, *Speculum historiale* 4.109. I have used MS B. N. lat. 4897.
7. See John J. Savage, "Medieval Traditions of Cerberus," *Traditio* 7 (1949–51): 405–10.

Following this, the Anonymous again tells the Tantalus legend, this time
using the interpretations of William or of Nicholas Trevet, who pretty
much agree. For the succeeding fifty-line story of Tytius, however, the
Anonymous undoubtedly relied on Trevet's account, which stresses
Apollo's punishment of Tytius for the folly of his attempted divination.
Finally, the translator returns to Orpheus for thirty-two concluding lines
which lightly finish with a musical lesson:

> Et ensy pert li homes sa paine,
> Qui plus estudie et se paine
> De consonances de musique
> Ramener a arismetique;
> Meïsmement a dire de fait
> Pourquoy quelque accorde se fait
> D'une note a l'autre et s'affiere
> D'un teil son non d'aultre maniere;
> Dont qui plus le quiert en appert
> Comme Orpheüs sa femme il le pert.

[fol. 53]

While it is obvious from this summary that the Anonymous's account
of the Orpheus legend and associated matters is indeed repetitive, two
things ought to be observed. The first is that the translator is quite aware
of the structure of his narrative. In the telling of the judgment of Paris, for
example, he looks both behind and ahead to related details in other parts
of his book: "Mais quant a ore m'en delivre / Car dit en ay ou premier livre
/ Qui fu Venuz et de quel pere," and twenty-four lines later, "Paris / Qui
puis fu Helaine maris / Sicom je le propose a mettre / Ou quart livre et ou
darrain metre." Similarly, he notes Boethius's discussion of themes relative
to the Orpheus fable when he says, apropos the devil's gifts, "Boeces
chartre / En son tierche livre est fair memore / Dignités, richés, et glore."
Further, it should be observed that the Anonymous is quite conscious of
his audience and the limits of their tolerance for digression and moralization. He clearly marks for them the transitions from tale to morality: "Et
atant fine la parole / Tantalus en grec parabole / Mais quant attient a moral
sench," and later when he introduces his remarks on music, "Et qui par
plus soubtil maistrie / Voelt dire par allegorie." Having just related the
story of Arion, he returns to Orpheus with this remark, "Mais il est boin
qu'je me taise / Que mes lons parlers ne desplaise / Et a Orpheüs me
radreche." And he anticipates our pleasure in the story of the judgment of
Paris:

> Et cest che que l'ystoire dist
> Se souffise quand a mon dit,
> Mais pou solas un petit faire
> Voel de .iii. dieuesses retraire.

Another aspect of the Anonymous's solicitousness for his readers is his frequent citation of authorities, even those he does not really use. Before showing the one important effect this has, I should perhaps instance a couple of examples of this contrived scholarship. Although the Anonymous clearly indicates his reliance on Fulgentius, he goes on to cite second-hand the long-lost sources that Fulgentius himself had cited: "Sicom Dromotrides retraite," and "Dont Batinius soloit dire." He does the same when introducing the story of Arion, without mentioning this time that he found it all in the encyclopedia of Vincent of Beauvais, "Que recorde Helinans et dist / Et Agilles en un sien dit." Whatever his motive for this sort of mild deception (one in which Chaucer, too, notoriously indulged), the allusions of the Anonymous do call our attention to the main cause for the repetitiveness that characterizes his account, namely his obvious allegiance to the tradition of scholastic interest in mythic polyvalence.

In broad outline, what the Anonymous of Meun seems to have done was draw in turn on Fulgentius's *Mithologiae,* Vincent of Beauvais's *Speculum historiale,* and a gloss on the *Consolatio*—probably some MS compilation of the glosses of William of Conches and Trevet. Instead of attempting to harmonize their accounts, however, the Anonymous simply exhausted the interest that each had for him and then moved on. The kind of use he made of Vincent, furthermore, seems to have been dictated in part by the fortuitous appearance of Boethius's name in the encyclopedia. Thus, because Vincent noted that Boethius mentioned both Arion and Orpheus in his discourse on music, the Anonymous acquired one reason for interpolating the story of Arion into his translation. Of course there are deeper affinities between the tales of Arion and Orpheus, but Vincent probably supplied the original suggestion for the Anonymous's associating them.

Although the original assembly of these diverse materials may have been motivated by scholastic affection for polyvalence, the product of their combination has the effect of invalidating for the translations another of Jeauneau's observations about the commentaries. And that is his assertion that the allegorical significance of all three heroic figures—

Ulysses, Orpheus, and Hercules—is the same: a presentment of *Sapience*.[8]
It is true that William identifies Orpheus as the sage and eloquent man, and
this is reflected in the portrait drawn by the author of the earliest prose
translation. But something quite different emerges from the translation
just surveyed. As the Anonymous of Meun begins to multiply and elaborate on the sinful characters inhabiting hell, our interest turns to them and
especially to the variety of reasons for their presence there. And as he
elaborates on Orpheus as a failed contemplative, we can begin to discern in
the whole collection of these persons something of a typical medieval
panorama of the deadly sins. In Ixion we see the prideful seeker of
personal glory; in Tantalus both the angry and the covetous man; and in
the first Tytius, the lustful man guilty also of vaunting pride, while in the
second Tytius, we have a more complex kind of Faustian pride in his
knowledge and ability to prophesy. Where in this spectrum lies the sin of
Orpheus?

Our first comparative glimpse comes in the characterization of Arion
as a figure puzzled by his good fortune:

> Aryons en la cité monte
> Tous soels, tous moulliés, tous emplus,
> Pensis, merveilleus, et tresplus
> De ce que li ere avenu;
> Et comment Diex l'avoit tenu
> Sans perir en mer et empris
> S'en estoit de paour espris.

[fol. 50]

The Anonymous does not allegorize Arion's story, but it makes a good
comparison with that of Orpheus, who also cannot understand the effect
his music has on nature. But in Orpheus's case the result is lamentable,
because while all nature is soothed by his song, he is powerless to help
himself: "Il remanoit tristes et mas." And a similar portrait emerges from
the contrasting story of the judgment of Paris. Where Hercules opts for the
active life—a taste for which he inherited from Juno—and Paris chooses the
blandishments of Venus, Orpheus is exhibited as too passive and enervated
to concentrate on the gift of Pallas: a life of disinterested contemplation
of such things as the music and mathematics exalted earlier. Thus, I think
it is possible to see in Orpheus a victim of the medieval equivalent of the
Boethian disease itself: the sin of *acedia*.

8. Jeauneau, p. 40.

Concerning the kind of reallegorizing I am attempting here, Siegfried Wenzel offers a valid caution in his study of *acedia*. In Wenzel's view, it might be justifiable to identify the Anonymous of Meun's portrait of Orpheus with the concept of sloth only if "the allegorized concept does not stand in a vacuum but is linked to other allegorized concepts in a fashion that corresponds with a clearly recognizable and coherent pattern of medieval thought."[9] I think this demand can be satisfied, because the pattern of thought here emerges from two directions. In the sequence of equivalents of pride, anger, lust, and avarice that we see in the repeated portraits of Ixion, Tantalus, and Tytius, the association of Orpheus with *tristitia* and *torpor animi* allows us to fill the gap left for a victim of sloth; and, secondly, the positive portraits of Hercules, Paris, and the lucky Arion deepen by contrast the sad passivity of Orpheus.

Where William of Conches allegorized out of existence the patent and miserable defeat of Orpheus in Hades, the Anonymous of Meun, then, found in his miscellaneous materials the makings of a portrait of Boethian sloth. Thus the narratives based on the elaboration of the *Consolatio* by the Latin commentaries occasionally came to ignore the associated allegorical interpretations, because the fictive details accumulated by the translators were more easily structured by popular medieval schemata—such as the seven deadly sins—than by those arguments of interest to Neoplatonists.

I think this interpretation of the significance of the Orpheus legend is retained in the much-revised copy that appears in the only other manuscript of the version by the Anonymous of Meun: B. N. fr. 1543. Concerning this MS, Antoine Thomas notes only that it contains a great many changes in texture from MS B. N. fr. 576 and that it has a large gap in its narration of the Orpheus passage. But the MS, so far from being negligible, is remarkable, I believe, and that for the evidence it offers of a real attempt at significant structural revision of the story so as to eliminate the very repetitiveness to which Thomas objected.

The gap Thomas refers to occurs as a blank space left on the vellum

9. Siegfried Wenzel, *The Sin of Sloth: Acedia in Medieval Thought and Literature* (Chapel Hill, 1967), p. 127. At least one medieval French poem associates Orpheus with *acedia*, but Jean de Courcy's *Le Chemin de Vaillance* takes the search for Eurydice to be an exemplum of Diligence, the opposite of *acedia* (p. 241). But Grosseteste saw *curiositas* (like a backward glance?) as a sinful excess of Diligence, so perhaps the appearances are saved (pp. 226–7).

amounting to a loss of some 215 lines from the copy in MS 576. This loss may reflect a gap in the scribe's exemplar, or, if he is the revisor too, it may indicate a judgment about the relevance of the matter contained in the passage. That is, he may have decided that the story of Arion and some of the following matter on Calliope was of sufficient tangency to allow him to go on with the rest of the Orpheus story and return if time permitted. Other conjectures are of course possible, but it is the substantive revision of the latter part of the Orpheus material that is of greatest interest.

Before the large gap, this second MS lacks only eight lines from the copy in MS 576—except for initial lost folios—but after the gap the compression is considerable. The second telling of the Ixion legend is cut from fifty-six to eight lines with the remark, "duquel ja avons fait memore." Following the story of the judgment of Paris, the final remarks on Ixion, Tantalus, and that part on Tytius not taken from Nicholas Trevet are cut from forty-eight to twelve lines. The two sections of new matter, however, are treated more cautiously. The judgment of Paris is reduced from 170 to 124 lines, the main deletions being details about Pallas's astronomical knowledge and the bulk of Venus's prize-winning speech to Paris. Only four lines are dropped from the final relation on Tytius, and these do not affect the new interpretation derived from Trevet. In all, the repetitive second half of the Orpheus meter is reduced by some 130 lines without significant loss of detail important to our understanding of the perils of Orphic paralysis. The deduction to be made from all this is that some medieval editor attempted to overcome one of the structural defects of eclecticism by making a narrative of cleaner lines, and it was on rewriting the exclusively narrative passages that the revisor expended his greatest effort.

It is interesting to compare the amateurish structure of the Anonymous's version with the more skillful job in Robert Henryson's *Orpheus and Eurydice* (printed 1508).[10] This 633–line poem is written in three different meters. The first two-thirds of the poem consist of fifty-two seven-line stanzas devoted to a somewhat aureate narration of the legend. Into these are intruded five stanzas of ten lines each constituting a courtly "Complaint of Orpheus." The last third of the poem consists of 220 lines in couplets closely versifying parts of the commentary by Nicholas Trevet on Book III, meter 12, of the *Consolatio*.

10. See *The Poems and Fables of Robert Henryson,* ed. H. Harvey Wood, 2nd ed., rev., (Edinburgh, 1958), pp. 129–48.

The first narration has been adapted to the succeeding commentary by the inclusion of the Aristaeus episode and the naming of the Furies. Its other medieval features include the forementioned "Complaint," a two-stanza technical digression on music—"Thair leirit he tonis proportionat, / As duplare, triplare, and emetricus"—and a list of the sinful inmates of hell, e.g., "Alexander for his wrang conqueist," and "Herod with his brudiris wyfe." But the poem also contains several novel, though no less medieval, passages such as the opening genealogy of the Nine Muses and the celestial descent of Orpheus through the several Ptolomaic spheres.

Thus, though Henryson's poem may have been written as much as a century and a half after that of the Anonymous, and though its texture may show a renaissance glitter in its diction and prosody, the basic structure of the poem is profoundly medieval in its bifurcation, digressiveness, and polyvalence.[11]

When we narrow the focus from these structural matters to view the texture of the poem on Orpheus written by the Anonymous of Meun, we can see even more clearly how far we have come from an exclusive interest in moralization on the way to the delight in pure narrative exhibited by Renaut de Louhans. For example, William of Conches had supplied the Anonymous with the barest details of the fables of Ixion and the judgment of Paris. I quote a bit of the latter:

> Vnde in fabulis invenitur quod tres dee Iuno, Pallas, Venus iudicio Paridis que dignior esset aureo pomo quesierunt, quia Iupiter diffinire noluit. Quod non fuit aliud quod tres vite sunt, scilicet teorica id est contemplativa, practica id est activa, philargiria id est voluptaria. Et ponitur Pallas pro contemplativa, Iuno pro activa, Venus pro voluptaria. Quod potest probari per premia que promittuntur Paridi. Pallas namque promittit sapientiam quia contemplatione fit aliquis sapiens. Iuno divicias quia per activam vitam acquiruntur divicie. Venus promittit feminam quia in ea est maxima voluptas. Iste tres dee pro pomo certant, id est pro beatitudine, quia unaqueque videtur facere beatum. Sed Iupiter hoc noluit diffinire ne libertatem arbitrii videretur auferre. Vnde querunt iudicium Paridis, scilicet cuiuslibet hominis. Sed Paris adquiescit Veneri quia maxima pars hominum consentit voluptati.[12]

The Anonymous turns these details into a spirited debate among the three ladies for possession of the golden apple bearing the legend, "Je suis le plus belle des trois!" In that debate, Juno briefly offers Paris the world, but for Pallas the sky is the limit of her gift of knowledge:

11. A similar conclusion is reached by Gros Louis; see my note 3.
12. Quoted from Jeauneau, p. 52.

> Quel cose c'est dou firmament,
> De ses cours, de leur mouvement,
> Et en aprés des .vii. planettes
> De leurs erres et de leur mettes,
> Des elemens, des creatures
> Qui en sont en mainltes faitures.

But Dame Venus has the longest, most persuasive speech and the most insistent character. She begins with quiet laughter at the foolish remoteness of her rivals' gifts, bears down hard on the delights of the flesh, and ends with a naked threat to deny Paris those Hellenic pleasures that he has begun to anticipate. Paris responds by throwing the apple at her feet and pledging himself to her in perfect courtly homage. William of Conches had simply said that Paris chose Venus because men are like that, but the Anonymous of Meun creates both psychological motives and social sanctions for Paris's act.

In contrast, the version of the Orpheus meter by Renaut de Louhans represents the ultimate stage in the gradual rejection of explicit moralization in favor of the temptations of the integument, although it could have been written no more than two decades after the work of the Anonymous of Meun. Renaut's 184–line narration proceeds without digression or moralization through a neat succession of modestly elaborated episodes that follow Orpheus on his singing tour through this world and the nether one. The focus is always on the effects of Orpheus's music. Renaut's relation of Tytius, for example, tells us that the giant suffered "pour sa transgression" without hinting what that was. We are given instead a picture of the vulture raising its head at the sound of Orpheus's approaching music: "Pour la doulceur lieve sa teste / Et de menger tantost s'arreste." There is no explanation. The narrative is everything.

Renaut's Benedictine revisor wrote a new prologue and added some dozen lines according to his scholarly lights, pointing out that Orpheus was raised in Thrace in a part of Greece. The monk does make an interesting suggestion that Orpheus was an exponent of courtly love when he says that it is folly to make laws, "a fin amour / Car Orpheus fust amans fins," but he fails to develop this as Henryson was to do later, and he ends with a new epilogue of six lines emphasizing the pains of hell: "Ce püant venimeux gouffre / Ou sans fin art l'eternel souffre." Even with this tag, however, Renaut's relation of Orpheus remains what it was: pure integument, an unworn dress.

We have seen in the progress observed in this chapter something like a structural reflex of the situation described by Donald R. Howard in his study of Chaucer, Langland, and the *Pearl*-poet. There, it is argued, apropos of the development of courtly love, that "what the allegorists call cortex in the early writings . . . like the *De Amore* of Andreas, came in the later writings of the courtly tradition—for example, the sonnet sequence— to be in effect the nucleus,"[13] although images of Christian charity continue to be used by sonneteers long after their attention has shifted to the once-peripheral erotic situation. Somewhat similarly, in the translations of the *Consolatio,* we see first the detailed scholastic explication of Boethian allusion for the sake of allegorizing it, followed by the gradual disappearance of this interpretive "nucleus" in the verse translations. We have, in effect, the replacement of the allusive, rhetorical Boethian mode by an explicit, narrative one, after an hermeneutic interlude. The story of Orpheus had served Boethius as an exemplary allusion to the necessity for the good man to keep his eye on celestial things. Scholastic commentary explicated and rationalized the appearance of this pagan myth in its revered authority by allegorizing it, but medieval scholarship also contributed to the accumulation of additional narrative traditions. Given the translators' lack of interest in the former, it is the latter that survive. And it is possible that the resulting characteristics of the translators' versions— their dwindling allegorical content and their patchwork composition— themselves had an effect on later vernacular literature. Somehow Chaucer found it reasonable to associate Boethian views directly with pagan contexts and safely attribute whole or partial versions of his ideas on Fortune and Providence to such figures as Troilus and Theseus, while Henryson's poem, which focuses on the pagan myth and appends the translation of Trevet's commentary as a jingling afterthought, is characterized by Kenneth Gros Louis as the last mythological poem of the Middle Ages and the last to "contain so many discordant echoes."[14]

13. Donald R. Howard, *The Three Temptations: Medieval Man in Search of the World* (Princeton, 1966), pp. 38–9.
14. Gros Louis, p. 655. For a Latin precedent to pursuit of integument, see Marc– René Jung, *Études sur le poème allégorique en France au moyen âge,* Romanica Helvetica 82 (Berne, 1971), citing a 664-line poem that recounts the legend of Orpheus after a reduction to 242 lines of Martianus' huge *Marriage of Mercury and Philology*: "la signification de l'emprunt à Martianus Capella réside dans le fait que le poète anonyme s'en tient à la fable mythologique, à l'*écorce,* en dehors de toute implication cosmologique" (p. 45).

IV

A Legacy for Common Profit

Pour ce que scet bien mon entente
Jehan de Calais, honnorable homme,
Qui ne me vit des ans a trente
Et ne scet comment je me nomme,
De tout ce testament, en somme,
S'aucun y a difficulté,
L'oster jusque'au rez d'une pomme
Je luy en donne faculté.

De le glosser et commenter,
De le diffinir et descripre,
Diminuer ou augmenter,
De le canceller et prescripre
De sa main et ne sceut escripre,
Interpreter et donner sens,
A son plaisir, meilleur ou pire:
A tout cecy je m'y consens.

Villon, Le Testament, 1844–59

IN HIS LIBERAL BEQUEST to a man who had not seen him in thirty years and who had never known his name, Villon's irony crows, but the technical terms of that legacy bespeak something of the actual processes by which medieval literature was composed. In the discussion thus far we have seen some examples of that terminology in operation. When the medieval translators elaborated on the allusions to classical myth and history in the *Consolatio,* they were exercising their right to gloss and comment, define and describe, diminish or augment. In this final chapter we shall be looking at the ultimate stages of those processes heretofore discriminated, but the evidence will differ in two ways from that considered earlier. It will consist first of instances of alterations in form, as parts of the *Consolatio,* narrative or otherwise, were medievalized according to the canons of fourteenth-century poetics; and secondly, the evidence will

67

comprise much post-classical matter as medieval authors sought apt illustration for their new interpretations of Boethian themes.

Part of the process of medievalizing the *Consolatio* consisted in submitting this valued text to the currents of poetic experimentation run-
ning so strongly through the century of Machaut and Deschamps. While
the earliest translations in French were exclusively in prose, even the first
of them recognized the value of Boethius's meters by repeating, as we have
seen, the commentators' cliché that he was not only the equal of Cicero in
prose but also of Virgil in verse. The meters had received continuous
attention, of course, throughout the Middle Ages, both from scholars and
poets. They formed, in fact, the exclusive topic of the earliest commentary, that by Lupus of Ferrières (mid–9th century).[1] And, while many of
the Latin commentators continued to use and revise the work of Lupus, a
new commentary devoted solely to the metrics was written in the early
Renaissance by Niccolo Perotti, archbishop of Siponto, in which he
compared the prosodies of Horace and Boethius.[2] As for the poets, King
Alfred cast into formulaic, alliterative verse the proper passages in his
prose translation,[3] and at the latter end of the Middle Ages, interest in the
Boethian medley was still so strong that an early print of one of the
French translations claims to include a version of the *Aeneid* in alternating
prose and verse.[4] But it is in the French translations themselves that we
see the most intense concern with the possibilities of Boethian metrics.

While the translator of the first mixed version restricted his verses to
octosyllabic couplets, his revisor experimented with Alexandrines arranged
into monorimed stanzas when he recast the translation of Book I, meter 5,
"O stelliferi." I give the first of these stanzas:

> Tu qui les estoiles mises ou firmament
> Et te siez en ton throsne sans nul esmouvement
> Et faiz tourner le ciel tost et ysnellement,
> Les estoiles gouvernes a ton commendement.
> Ore est plaine la lune, ore est en defaillement
> Et Lucifer l'estoile alume clerement.
> Or la fin de l'advent, or le commandement,

1. Text in R. Peiper's ed. of the *Consolatio* (Leipzig, 1871), pp. xxxiv–xxxviii.
2. Niccolo Perotti, *Epistola de generibus metrorum quibus Horatius Flaccus et S.
   Boetius usi sunt* (n.p., 1471).
3. Larry D. Benson, "The Literary Character of Anglo–Saxon Formulaic Poetry,"
   PMLA 81 (1966):334–41.
4. *Gesamtkatalog der Wiegendrucke* (Leipzig, 1930), vol. 4, no. 4577.

Or sont les jours en croys or en descroyssement
Le temps de l'an devises moult ordeneement
En autompne cheent fueilles, en printemps vont germant
Or recoyt on les blez, or les va l' en semant.

[N.L.W. 5039, fol. 13]

This revision may stand as a sign of the times, for the only translations to be restricted to single metrical schemes throughout the text were the first mixed version and that by the Anonymous of Meun, and the latter, as we have seen, enormously elaborated his version in other ways.

In his wholly verse translation, Renaut de Louhans used eight-line stanzas for his prologue and Book I—except for one meter—and then changed to couplets for Books II through V, again with the exception of two stanzaic interpolations. In his interpretation of the second meter of Book I, Renaut experimented by turning it into six twelve-line stanzas riming *a a b a a b b b a b b a*.[5] Of Renaut's three revisors, each one recast this meter, at least partially, into a different verse form, and the MSS of the Benedictine's revision show two traditions. A closer look at these variations will, I hope, demonstrate the vitality of formal experimentalism as an aspect of medievalization as well as show the diverse effects of such efforts on the Boethian meaning.

For the epitome in MS B. N. fr. 25418, the revisor picked some thirty-two lines out of Renaut's stanzas and linked them largely into couplets, except for Renaut's fifth stanza which appears to have been abbreviated in the spirit of his customary eight-liner. The reflexes of Book I, meter 2, in MSS of the Benedictine's revision of Renaut are much more complex. I see three states. The first, represented in the Bibliothèque Nationale by MSS 12237 and 12240, is a complete retranslation of the meter in seven of Renaut's normal eight-line stanzas and a final one of eleven lines. The second, and most common, state is represented by MSS B. N. fr. 577, 812, 813, 1094, 12238, 12239, 25416, and nou. acq. fr. 1982. This state is like the first except that it reduces the first two stanzas to six lines each by simple omission of lines. The third state is actually a compilation occurring only, to my knowledge, in MS B. N. fr. 12459.[6] It is like the Benedictine's first state but after the second stanza adds two eight-line stanzas mechani-

---

5. See A. Bernhardt, *Die altfranzösisch Helinandstrophe* (Münster, 1912).
6. This MS is mentioned in the final footnote to Leopold Delisle, "Anciennes traductions françaises de la Consolation de Boèce conservée à la Bibliothèque Nationale," *Bibliothèque de l'École des Chartes* 34 (1873):32.

cally reduced from Renaut's stanzas two and three, and after the final stanza of the Benedictine's version it simply attaches the last thirty lines of Renaut's translation. Finally, the second mixed version, compiled from a revision of the Benedictine's verses and an original translation of the prose, in the case of this meter rewords and rearranges lines somewhat for the first nineteen lines and then reproduces the remainder of the Benedictine's version in its second state.

Before turning to the effect of all this revision on meaning, I would point out that the boldness of Renaut's original experiments, imitated to some extent by the Benedictine, is clearly countered by the conservatism of manuscript processes which attempt to regularize Renaut's forms in the direction of one or the other of his customary meters. This is a tiny instance of the very general medieval situation which I would call the socialization of creativity. As successive scribes and their managers produce successive "performances" of each literary work, their tendency is to smooth out the text, to eliminate eccentricity, and, in effect, to reduce or elevate all literature to a common standard. In such an environment it is not necessarily so that genius is an asset nor origin in an uncouth province a liability, for the odder effects of both may be eliminated.

The failure of Renaut's stanzas here to conform to his general practice was only one of the revisors' motives for redoing the translation of Book I, meter 2. The Benedictine, at least, seems to have been offended by Renaut's violation of the original structure of the Boethian verse. Boethius's poem is curious, for it presents but a single contrast in a three-part structure. Five introductory lines on the narrator's present misery are followed by eighteen lines celebrating his former intellectual achievements, and four concluding lines recall us to his current mindless stupor. By contrast, in each of Renaut's six stanzas, Philosophy both celebrates and laments Boethius's two moods, often as the protasis and apodosis of a single sentence: "Cilz qui rendoit raison et cause / De toute chose haulte et basse / Maintenant a raison perdue." A second feature of Renaut's version is that it largely ignores the rich details of the central praise of intellectual beauty. The Benedictine's stanzas attempt to remedy both of these novelties, and he produces, I think a successful evocation of the Boethian original:

> Aussi discerne il proprement
> Qui cause en printemps le doulx vent,
> Dont la terre est toute florie
> Et aournée cointement
> Des roses . . .

The abbreviation in MS B. N. fr. 25418, on the other hand, by cutting out alternate lines, managed to make of Renaut's version an almost exclusively morbid poem. And this effect is in keeping with the generally glum cast of this version, which also eliminates almost all of Philosophy's positive vision in Book V. Its author was more monk than *philosophe.*

In contrast with these simplifying efforts, we can see in the verses made by the translator of Colard Mansion's 1477 print several bold attempts to match the prosodic variety of the Latin model as he used couplets of varied lengths and some stanzaic patterns. The translator's version of the final meter of Book I, for example, successfully imitates for forty lines the five-syllable scansion of his model:

> Estoille mucée
> De noire nuée
> Nullement ne donne
> Sur nous sa lumiere;
> Se la mer tournée
> Auster moult meslée
> Chaleur fort foisonne,
> L'eau de maniere.

[fol. 38v]

For the opening meter of Book II, the translator wrote six stanzas on the following complex pattern:

> Quant Fortune la diverse
> Ses offices change ou verse,
> Comme Euripus se reverse
> En s'eschauffant fort bouillonne
> Toult et donne.

[fol. 41v]

And, finally, he ventured thirty-two long, and suitably epic, lines for his version of Book IV, meter 3:

> Quant le duc Ulixes se retournoit de Troye,
> Aprés qu'il eut perdu par mer ses gens, sa proye,
> Droit en l'isle ou Circe demouroit print sa voye.

[fol. 103]

As a final example of the sort of formal experimentation that contributed to the medievalization of Boethius, we may turn to another of the results of the manuscript process of compilation, because works that surround, and in this case mingle with, the Boethian text may relate to contemporary interpretation of it in the same way that a modern edition influences its readers in some degree by the editor's notes. In the curious Trinity Hall MS, Camb. 12—already remarked—we find a number of ballades interspersed between the latter books of the *Consolatio* and following works. One of these ballades has a refrain, "Je meurs de soif auprès de la fontaine," which provides the line later chosen by Charles d'Orléans as the theme of his poetic "Concours de Blois."[7] The poem would have additional significance in the Boethian context if it were the case, as Philippe Ménard asserts, that this theme is an outgrowth of the Tantalus legend.[8] The Benedictine's treatment of this legend in the translation that surrounds these poems might well have been cited by Ménard for the bearing some of its phrasing could have had on that of the ballade: e.g., "L'onde tantost arriere fuit / Ainsi meure de soif jour et nuit." In the context of this discussion, however, these interpolated ballades provide but one more example of the range of metrical exploration that medieval authors were willing to associate with the Boethian text, making it resemble such avant-garde works as Machaut's *Remède de fortune* with its interpolated ballades in a medley of dialogue and verse.[9] Certainly no other medieval translation was so honored by being so formally medievalized.

When we move from these formal details to look at the last phases of the medieval conquest of the content of the *Consolatio,* the record becomes that of an inevitable failure on the one hand and on the other of a convincing victory; because while the translators were only slightly more successful than the commentators in Christianizing this work, they were able to universalize much of its message.

Although there is adequate evidence that Boethius was a Christian, commentators on the *Consolatio* since the earliest Carolingian glossators have been troubled by its lack of Christian focus or, indeed, reference. Pierre Courcelle has convincingly argued the decent compatibility of these facts by showing that although the *Consolatio* belongs to the ancient genre of the apocalypse, its revelations concern exclusively human wisdom, perfected in Neoplatonism and personified in Lady Philosophy. This explains her silence on matters of divine revelation:

7. R. A. Dwyer, " 'Je meurs de soif auprès de la fontaine,' " *French Studies* 23 (1969):225–8.

8. Philippe Ménard, "Je meurs de soif auprès de la fontaine: d'un mythe antique à une image lyrique," *Romania* 87 (1966):394–400.

9. In *Oeuvres,* ed. E. Hoepffner, Société des anciens textes français (Paris, 1911), vol. 2.

Elle ne peut, par sa nature propre, dépasser le point de vue rationnel; quand Boèce lui demandera s'il y a des châtiments après la mort, elle refusera de s'engager sur ce sujet. Il est donc naturel qu'elle ne cite pas l'Écriture, qu'elle ignore les théologiens. Que Boèce soit chrétien ou non, toute allusion à l'Écriture ou aux théologiens aurait été, après qu'il eut choisi ce personnage fictif de Philosophie, une faute de logique et de goût. Son silence n'est pas une négation.[10]

This explication would not, of course, have satisfied most medieval commentators, who attempted in various ways to Christianize Boethian views, particularly those on cosmology, the eternity of the world, and the pre-existence of souls. Their efforts ranged from the Eriugenan brink of heresy in accepting the *Consolatio* to the patronizing Aristotelian rejection of it by late medieval scholastics, and I refer those interested in the details of the process to Courcelle's expert account. What is relevant to our argument is that these attempts to Christianize the doctrine of the *Consolatio* failed to persuade contemporaries. To the extent that the translators followed the model of the commentators, they too failed. What modest success they did achieve came about solely through the subversive effect of assumed Christian ethic in their narratives.

Both of the translations which take their glosses from William of Conches represent serious efforts to bring into the vernacular certain explicitly Christian interpretations of problematical doctrine in the *Consolatio*. In addition, the earliest translation draws upon the Christianizing tenth-century commentary of Adalbold of Utrecht for its gloss on Book III, meter 9. Neither of these efforts could be successful, of course, for any large appeal to Christ's redemptive mission immediately renders supererogatory all of Boethius's injunctions concerning the power of human reason to comprehend man's fate. Such direct appeals are, in fact, only slightly subtler rejections of the Boethian position than that achieved by Bonaventura da Demena in the following announcement of certain interpolations in his translation: "l'auctor de ceste translacions veut ici moustrer les .x. comandamenz de la loi divine et les generals comandamenz de la dileccions de Deu et del prosme qi se treuvent en le Vielz Testament, et aucune doctrine des conseilz et de la profeccions del Nouvel Testament."[11] Bonaventura adds that Boethius left this matter out only because it is so well treated in Scripture. Such infrequent additions as

10. Pierre Courcelle, *La Consolation de philosophie dans la tradition littéraire* (Paris, 1967), p. 24.
11. MS B. N. fr. 821, fol. 38v.

these will not concern us, because they were unsuccessful as medievalizing agents and because they do not involve narrative.

The explicitly Christian allegorization of Boethian fable is of interest, however, because an author who says Ulysses reminds us of Christ may be more persuasive than one who simply contradicts Boethius. The earliest translation, in fact, makes some interesting parallels, as when it says that Ulysses returned home alone just as Christ left the Twelve behind, "for many are called, but few are chosen."

> Ce que nos avons dit par moralité pooms entendre par allegorie. Par Ulixes qui est estranges de toz, pooms entendre Jhesu Crist qui est veire sapience. Il vint a Troie, ce est en cest munde e venqui le deable e sez compaignons, e retorna par mer, ce est sofri maintes turbacions en cest siecle, e herberia en la maison de Circe, mais ne but pas de ses herbes. Ce est, Jhesu Crist fu veirs hom e fu entre les temporels ovres, mais non pecha. Il perdi moltz de ses compaignons poi en retornerent ensemble lui. Car l'Evangile le dit, "Moltz sunt apelé a la fei de Crist, mais poi sunt eslit."[12]

Perhaps more successful in giving at least a Christian tone to the *Consolatio* are those instances of the apt use of a Christian example where none at all exists in the Boethian text. In Book IV, prose 6, for example, Philosophy remarks that God's judgment is so delicate that He may spare a good man whom adversity might ruin and may not allow a man who cannot stand suffering to suffer, however instructive it might be for others. No example is adduced, doubtless because the annals of Rome are not crowded with hypersensitive heroes, but the glossator of the revised mixed version found a touching medieval example in William of Conches and used it, shorn of all scholastic comment:

> Note ce que l'en list en la vie de Saint Julien comme l'en le traisnast et menast en la prison d'un tyrant vint un sien filz qui par l'inspiracion divine creoit en Jhesu Crist et suyvoit le martyr de Dieu et fut mis avec luy en la prison, et depuis converti sa mere a la foy de Notresire. Et quant le tyrant le sceut, il fist occire son filz et commanda que on lui amenast la mere pour la faire mourir, mais ceulx qui la vouloient prendre ne povoient et perdoyent le povoir des mains, car Dieu qui sçauvez la vouloit, savoit bien qu'elle ne pouvroit endurez les tourmens, mais quant elle eut dicté son oraison, elle trespassa en Notresire.[13]

12. MS Vienna 2642, fols. 60v–61.
13. MS Nat. Lib. of Wales 5039, fol. 60. In Remigius; see *Acta Sanctorum* Jan. 1, 580–85.

While Boethius's Latin commentators could not wrestle his Neoplatonic doctrines into submission to dogma, his French translators could at least quietly infiltrate the exclusively pre-Christian ranks of his examples. By doing so they make both truth and illustration more familiar, while extending to the Boethian deity such qualities as compassion.

This non-discursive sort of Christianization of the text is also achieved to a lesser extent by the illustrators, and I will call attention to but a single example that Courcelle also notes.[14] Rouen MS 3045 contains a copy of Renaut de Louhans's verse version of the *Consolatio.* Placed at the end of Renaut's 500–line expansion of Book IV, meter 7—devoted mostly to the labors of Hercules—is a miniature showing Boethius being conducted to heaven by Lady Philosophy (fig. 6). He is adorned with the philosophic wings that the Lady was shown giving him in a previous icon. Above them, two angels point to the figure of God, who is pronouncing a blessing. The illustration, in effect, explicitly Christianizes the concluding lines of meter 7, which are inset into the picture, and, in consequence, their classical myth of Hercules' apotheosis:

> Et quant assés fut travaillie
> Avec les dieux fut essaucie.
> Alez donc les fors par proësce
> Ou bon example vous adresce,
> Et veez que cilz vont requerre
> Le ciel qui ont vaincu la terre.

It is in the translators' efforts to universalize the message of the *Consolatio,* however, that they made it most medieval. By universalization I mean the extension of the text to new and larger audiences through an increased range of tones and points of view,[15] and preliminary to a demonstration of this extension we need some idea of the limits placed on tone and audience by the original work. I have already cited Courcelle's observation that Boethius's use of *satura* excluded the customary cynicism

14. Courcelle, pp. 197–8 and pl. 122.
15. This is not identical to popularization. To cite the opinion of C. S. Lewis again, the medieval code of courtly love, for example, "in spite of all its shabby origins and pedantic rules, is at bottom more agreeable to those elements in human, or at least European, nature, which last longest, than the cynical Latin gallantries of Boccaccio. The world of Chrestien, of Guillaume de Lorris, and of Chaucer, is nearer to the world universal, is less of a closed system, than the world of Ovid, of Congreve, of Anatole France," and, *mutatis mutandis,* of Boethius. C. S. Lewis, "What Chaucer Really Did to *Il Filostrato,*" *Essays and Studies* 17 (1932):75.

and obscenity. In fact, he all but excludes everything unsolemn. Boethius does tell one joke (Bk. II, pr. 7) about how a true philosopher discomfited an imposter, but the original text of the *Consolatio* contains nothing like the range of indelicate detail the translators found for even those classical stories we have already noticed. In this, the translators were like the mendicant John Ridevall in following St. Augustine's approval of harsh satiric remedies: "Illi enim poete romanorum, quos vocabunt satiricos, fuerunt fortes et acuti reprehensores vitiorum et carnalium delectationum, sicut patet in libris Iuvenalis et Persii et poete Oratii."[16] When they added non-classical matter, the translators brewed a stronger potion still.

The extent to which Boethian tones are limited by his presumed audience has never been sufficiently stressed. For the group to which not only the *Consolatio* but the theological tractates was addressed was aristocratic and educated. When Philosophy is first introduced among the poetical muses standing by Boethius's bed, she becomes inflamed with anger at their presumption in trying to console a graduate of the academy: "At si quem profanum, uti uulgo solitum uobis, blanditiae uestrae detraherent, minus moleste ferendum putarem; nihil quippe in eo nostrae operae laederentur" (Bk. I, pr. 1:35–8). On all those other profane fellows she would not waste her time. This elitism is to be seen most dramatically, however, in the introduction to the tract *De Trinitate* which I quote from the Loeb translation:

> For, apart from yourself [Symmachus], wherever I turn my eyes, they fall on either the apathy of the dullard or the jealousy of the shrewd, and a man who casts his thoughts before the common herd—I will not say to consider but to trample under foot, would seem to bring discredit on the study of divinity. So I purposely use brevity and wrap up the ideas I draw from the deep questionings of philosophy in new and unaccustomed words which speak only to you and to myself, that is, if you deign to look at them. The rest of the world I simply disregard: they cannot understand, and therefore do not deserve to read.[17]

There is no stronger justification for the medieval philosophers' metaphor of unveiling truth than this statement of method by one engaged in wrapping up his pearls, and there can be no better immediate antidote to this

16. Ridevall on *De civ. Dei,* quoted in Beryl Smalley, *English Friars and Antiquity in the Early Fourteenth Century* (Oxford, 1960), p. 319.
17. *Boethius: The Theological Tractates,* ed. and trans. H. F. Stewart and E. K. Rand, Loeb Classical Library (Cambridge, Mass., 1918), p. 5.

elitism than to show how the homely fables in the version of Pierre de Paris both accommodate and extend Boethian truths.

In the first of these little tales, in fact, Pierre catches Philosophy in the act of having wrapped up nothing. She had just stated (Bk. III, pr. 12) that evil is nothing, since God, who can do all things, cannot do evil. At this point Boethius accuses her of weaving labyrinthine arguments, and the remainder of their dialogue concerns varieties of proof. Where the translator of the earliest French version chose to explicate *labyrinth,* Pierre innocently asks what has become of the question about whether God can do evil, and after giving his own answer that it is not the fact of evil that is important but the intent behind the act, Pierre adduces a little story which he says he found in the *Vies des Pères.* It concerns a hermit who gave penance to a murderous thief on condition that he restrain himself whenever he heard churchbells. The thief continued in his evil ways until one day, while in the act of assaulting a merchant, he heard the bells. The thief gave up his attack and tried to flee, but the merchant, believing that he had vanquished the thief, chased him and killed him. The text continues:

> L'ermite si vi en celuy point l'arme dou malfaitor que les angles portoient droytement au ciel; et sur ce merveilla molt l'ermite et se despera et dist que il avoit .xxx. ans et plus esté en l'ermitage [et] n'avoit pas encore veu nulle grace que Dieu il eust faite en ensi grant tens come il avoit esté et demoré en penanse; si se parti del hermitage et fu condampné, et le larron fu sauvé, qui faizoit les mauvaises euvres.[18]

We thus pass from the lofty position of Boethian logic that the perfect deity can author no evil to the ethical mystery of his power to detect the saving spark in thieves and murderers, and we similarly pass from Roman notions of human virtue to one that sees it as essentially non-public and apolitical. Needless to say, there are no such obscure, holy sinners among Boethius's exemplary patricians.

Another affecting example occurs in Pierre's amplification of Book II, prose 1, which concerns the fidelity of Fortuna to her mutable nature: "Tu [Boethius] fortunam putas erga te esse mutatam; erras. Hi semper eius mores sunt ista natura. Seruauit circa te propriam potius in ipsa sui muta-

18. MS Vat. lat. 4788, fol. 67v. Also printed in Antoine Thomas, "Notice sur le MS. 4788 du Vatican," *Notices et extraits de MSS de la Bibliothèque Nationale* 41 (1917):68–9. This tale is reminiscent of the popular medieval story of Eppo the thief; see J. Crosland, *Medieval French Literature* (Oxford, 1956), p. 124.

bilitate constantiam" (28–31). Into this elevated and abstract discourse, Pierre intrudes the oriental fable of the cat and the candle, which he mistakenly attributes to Marie de France:

> Et auci de .i. chat, se il avenist qu'acun per son engin se feist servir a .i. chat en aucun office, si come en tenir une chandele ardant, si come l'en raconte en les fables que une feme fist; et si avenist par aucune aventure que, en celuy point que le chat tenroit celle chandele, il veist .i. rat passer par devant soy, certes ce celuy chat getast le chandele et corust aprés le rat, nul ne se devroit merveiller, car tele est sa nature, ne de riens ne l'auroit changée.[19]

In this comic picture of the once obedient little cat flinging aside his appointed candle to chase a rat, Pierre strikes a note characteristic of Gothic naturalism. The same may be said of the literal miniaturization achieved in his borrowed story of the pygmies and cranes: "En celes montaignes habitent une maniere de gent molt petis, et sont si petis que le greignor de touz n'est que de .i. paume lonc; et se combatent as grues," and so on. Such stories recast Boethian solemnity into household figurines, redirect Boethian themes, and expand their application to include homely, pedestrian contexts. A sort of democratization of the aristocratic doctrine ensues and produces a two-way effect. The less than noble are introduced to the virtues of stoicism, and the stoics are humanized. We can see a splendid example of this latter effect in Pierre's treatment of the allusion to Alcibiades.

The long process by which François Villon came to include one *Archipiada* among his list of vanished beauties has been well charted from its origins in Carolingian glosses on the *Consolatio*.[20] Boethius had cited a lost work of Aristotle's which said that if men had the penetrating vision of Lynceus the Argonaut, they could see through Alcibiades' fair exterior to the vile entrails within (Bk. III, pr. 8). To tender medieval minds, fair bodies belonged to women, and details about this new female Alcibiades began to accumulate in glosses to the Boethian text. At the same time legends were growing about the medieval Aristotle, too, and with more point. Henri d'Andeli, who, like John of Garland, carried into the thir-

<hr>

19. Thomas, p. 53.
20. See Antoine Thomas and Mario Roques, "Traductions françaises de la *Cons. Phil. de Boèce*," in *Hist. litt. de la France* (Paris, 1938), 37:448; Ernest Langlois, "Archipiada," *Mélanges de philologie romane dediés à Carl Wahlund* (Mâcon, 1896), pp. 173–9; and Pierre Courcelle, pp. 258–9 and 280.

teenth century the older defence of school *auctores* against the champions
of the new Aristotelian logic, wrote the timely, iconoclastic *Lai d'Aristote*
(ca. 1250), in which Alexander's mistress tricks the lovesick Aristotle into
submitting to saddle and bridle and allowing her to ride him into the
presence of his royal pupil.[21] Pierre de Paris's ingenious contribution was
to identify that mistress with Alcibiades, which, to long memories of
Socrates' choice of companions, is witty. Pierre also adapted the story to
the context of Book III, prose 8—which scoffs at men's inability to be
stronger than bulls or swifter than tigers—by signaling Aristotle's metamor-
phosis: "et il chaitif estoit a .iiii. piés auci come une beste mue." And
finally, he changed the end of the story, which turned on the apt answer
of Aristotle to the obvious charges. In Henri's lai, Aristotle had remarked
pithily that if one so wise as himself could tumble, his lusty master ought
to take double care. Pierre changed this to the remark about Lynceus's
vision, except that by now the commentators had made Lynceus into a
Lynx. In both stories professional wisdom wins the day, but the medieval
Aristotle and Alcibiades are far more engaging persons than their austere
antique incarnations, and, as a consequence, their virtue, like that of Sir
Gawain after the Green Knight's test, is more credible because it has been
proved fallible.

Even more effectively than Pierre, Renaut de Louhans questioned the
unrelieved solemnity and rigor of Boethius's intellectual stand. Renaut
drew on Nicholas Trevet's commentary on the mid-thirteenth-century
Disciplina Scolarium and, as Astrik Gabriel has shown, on the commentary
of the Pseudo-Thomas on the *Consolatio,* for a comic story that Gabriel
calls "The Inconstant Scholar," about a young man who restlessly turned
from one calling to another, deciding in turn *not* to be a clerk, merchant,
farmer, knight, lawyer, bridegroom, or astronomer.[22] He finally settled
for being an ass: "Asnes ne met riens en sa teste / De riens au monde ne li
chaut / Autant du froit come de chaut." The account is, of course, satirical, as Renaut elaborated its sketches of the most uncomfortable features
of each calling: the teacher's unruly pupils, the merchant's dangerous
voyages, the fiancée's prodigality, and so forth. This aspect Professor

<hr>

21. Text in Anatole de Montaiglon and Gaston Reynaud, eds., *Recueil général et
    complet des fabliaux des XIIIe et XIVe siècles* (Paris, 1883), 5:243–62. This
    work also alludes to the story of the cat and the candle, lines 424–6.
22. Astrik L. Gabriel, "The source of the Anecdote of the Inconstant Scholar,"
    Classica et Medievalia 19 (1958):152–76.

Gabriel's article discusses in sufficient detail, and the value of the isolated tale for contemporaries is proven by its having been excerpted and circulated as a fabliau. What I would stress is the relevance of this interpolated story to the matrix of the *Consolatio.*

Inasmuch as it appears in Book II, prose 4, just after a biographical passage on Boethius, it might be argued that it contributes some desperately needed humor to the internal dynamics of the dialogue between the Lady and the Exile. In the scene before the fabliau, Philosophy has just conceded that Boethius's happiness about the fact that his wife still lives is somewhat marred since her sorrow for him is killing her. In the poem immediately following, the steady man is shown laughing at the elements. A comic tale inserted between the two could make this transition seem more probable. It should be admitted, however, that this aspect of the story's relevance is quite secondary.

Of far greater importance is the close connection between the theme and imagery of this tale and recurrent Boethian concerns. In this respect the final contrast of the fabliau is most significant. The last profession rejected by the scholar before he descends into assininity is that of astronomer, and the emphasis of the account is on the profound technical complexity of the subject. Having tried to master planetary motions both right and retrograde, the distinctions between fixed and erratic stars, poles arctic and antarctic, the mathematics of divisions, measurement and proportion, and the highest science of prognostication, our scholar "dit en sa melencolie / Que il vouldroit uns asne estre." The irony, it seems to me, is aimed as much at Boethius as anyone, for he again and again exhorts us to look up, behold the heavens, use dialectic and make ourselves free. But in the popular medieval imagination such interests are suspect, if not fatal, as the beguiled carpenter observes in Chaucer's *Miller's Tale*:

> Men sholde nat knowe of Goddes pryvetee.
> Ye, blessed be alwey a lewed man
> That noght but oonly his bileve kan!
> So ferde another clerk with astronomye;
> He walked in the feeldes, for to prye
> Upon the sterres, what ther sholde bifalle,
> Til he was in a marle-pit yfalle;
> He saugh nat that!

[lines 3454–61]

Renaut de Louhans's anecdote is not more anti-intellectual than Chaucer's, which goes back to Plato's *Theaetetus*; it is simply more skeptical than Boethius of the exclusively rational approach. And it is also far more tolerant than Boethius of the failure to succeed. As we saw in Book III, meter 2, and in the fable of Ulysses' companions, Boethius heaps scorn on any human yielding to the beast within, but Renaut is at least as concessive as a later Neoplatonist, Edmund Spenser, who found that the world had room to "Let Gryll be Gryll and have his hoggish mind."

The last illustration to be used in this study also comes from the translation of Renaut de Louhans, and it seems to me that it draws together many of the medievalizing forces, both formal and thematic, that have been discussed in this and the preceding chapters. Into his version of Book II, meter 7, Renaut interpolated some twenty stanzas of six lines each, riming *a a b a a b*. Their theme is seen in the first and last words of each of those stanzas: *La Mort.* Formally, they intrude on the customary couplets of this meter and signal their superior importance by their intricate pattern.[23] Like Renaut's experiment in Book I, meter 2, this formal nonconformity bothered the conservative scribes—B. N. fr. 19137, for example, rearranges the lines of the first five stanzas to rime *a a b b c c* to make them resemble the couplet pattern. But it is in the poem's treatment of its deadly theme that we can best see how far we have come from the Boethian meditation on mortality.

Book II, meter 7, focuses on the vanity and evanescence of earthly fame. No matter how great a man's fame, it will not spare him the fact of death. And since his renown will one day fade too, the great man is doubly doomed, because he will die a second death. For instances of those whom death has humbled, Boethius cites the consuls Fabricius, Lucius Junius Brutus, and the elder Cato. His illustration, as well as his audience, is clearly patrician.

Nicholas Trevet, Renaut's usual source for commentary, in this instance supplied him mainly with details about the careers of Fabricius, Brutus, and Cato. For the twenty stanzas which would extend both illustration and audience of Boethius's poem, Renaut turned therefore to a rich medieval tradition of images and gnomic sentiments on Death the Leveler, a tradition that had been growing since Hélinant, Cistercian monk of Froidmont, wrote his famous *Vers de la Mort* (ca. 1195).[24] Although

23. On Renaut's poem, see Thomas and Roques, p. 475, where earlier, fragmentary printings are noted.
24. *Les Vers de la mort par Hélinant,* ed. F. Wulff and E. Walberg, Société des

there are many similarities between the poems of Hélinant and Renaut, the Dominican does not follow his witty predecessor to his more hedonistic and un-Boethian conclusions:

> S'autres siecles n'est, donques viaus
> Ait ci li cors toz ses aviaus
> Et face quanque li delite:
> Vive li hom comme porciaus,
> Car toz pechiez est bon et biaus!
>
> [36, lines 1–5]

Renaut's poem begins with notice of the war Death has waged against humankind since Adam's outrage and continues with a crowded procession of its victims from all human estates. The clergy is fully represented, and the Christian infiltration of the aristocratic ranks of Boethian personnel becomes here a mortal rout of clerks, priests, cardinals, popes, prelates in furs, clergied canons, cloistered monks, and veiled nuns. Following them troup emperors, kings, dukes and counts, and knights-at-arms. Delicate glimpses succeed of "jeunes damoisiaux" whom death will seize despite their rings, whose pet birds, now playing on their fingers, will seek the woods when Death comes courting. Death robs the rich villain of his wine and bread, and pitilessly takes the husband of the burdened wife. Death comes to advocates despite their pleas, and to physicians for all their oaths. It comes en masse in plagues but stealthily to suicides. It is everywhere, in fields, woods, and parks; in town and court and countryside. It plies the seas to every port. It comes home to take the sucking babe. And last of all, Death was most bold and hardy in seizing Jhesu, "le Filz Marie," to whom we pray "Qu'il nous soit aidans en la vie / Et secours nous face a la mort."

Like his portrait of Fortune, Renaut's figure of Death is psychologized. Outraged, bold, and hardy, Death mocks his victims, saying to each, "Se tu m'eschapes / Tu serez moult pruez et fort!" Death, in fact, takes over the role of Fortune, and in this, Renaut's conception surpasses Boethius in a truly medieval contempt of the world and its goods, because where Fortune also gave, Death only takes. Fortune was subject to Providence because Boethian man was always free to ignore her goods, but Death requires everyone's attention.

---

anciens textes français (Paris, 1905). On the theme of Death, see the extensive citations in Italo Siciliano, *François Villon et les thèmes poétiques du moyen âge* (Paris, 1934), pp. 227–79.

The true universality of Renaut's poem, however, emerges from the range of Death's domain. Within his bending sickle's compass come all classes and estates, all earthly space, and all historical time from Adam to Christ to the very medieval audience which the poem addressed. And that audience included many an unpatrician face not the least illuminated by thought of earthly fame nor worried about any death but the first. Of course, the poem's last, least philosophic, and most universal irony is that, in the face of Death, the mercy of the Son of Mary is said to offer to men of all estates the best prospect of consolation.

But it is time to conclude. One persistent question about medieval culture concerns the relationship between the international world of Latin philosophy, theology, science, and art on the one hand and on the other the various popular vernacular literatures. A few writers like Dante and, on less exalted levels, Robert Grosseteste, Richard Rolle, John Gower, and Alain Chartier have provided answers of their own by writing in both Latin and the vernaculars and on a variety of topics; but their situations are untypical.

Recent explications of medieval literature reveal opposing views of the commerce between intellectual strata in the Middle Ages. We have, for example, the judgment of C. S. Lewis in *The Discarded Image* that the "Model" which served as a comfortable backdrop for most medieval fiction was a psychologically unified collection of scraps from the *Somnium Scipionis, The Divine Names,* and the like, to which Plato and Aristotle lent folklore on demons. A contrary view would deny the cultural dichotomy and regularly bring to discussions of what is at stake in the adventures of Beowulf and Chauntecleer the citation of patristic apologists and Carolingian postillators. The translations considered here provide novel testimony about just what kind of matter travelled down the medieval cultural scale.

The true medieval audience for the Latin *Consolatio* was academic, and through its interest in cosmology and technical questions of orthodoxy and authority it created a demand for copies of the text and commentaries. But the appeal of such matters to the vernacular audience was limited. Chaucer is a good example of the best lay audience for the *Consolatio,* and he accepted Jean de Meun's practice of distinguishing between translation and use. He adopted Jean's base for his own literal prose version, while poetically making a variety of fictional uses of the text in his original works. These range from the dramatic exploitation of half of the

Boethian argument on free will in characterizing Troilus[25] to the forceful recasting of Book II, meter 5, in "The Former Age." The first use is unfair to philosophy but makes good psychology, and the second is equally unacademic. But Chaucer was prepared to concede most Boethian technicalities upward to Bradwardine.

With the disintegration of the scholastic assumptions about the relevance of the *Consolatio,* copies, commentaries, and translations continued to be produced, but these last became accessible to other literary currents. The prime effect of its new academic status of obsolescent venerability was the liberation of the vernacular Boethius to poetic experimentation and narrative elaboration. Lesser authors than Jean and Chaucer applied their techniques not to original works but to the transmutation of a prestigious text. Without the pressure of academic assumptions about traditional distinctions between text and gloss, about canons of relevance in explications, and about adherence to a textual tradition, the translators played.

The earliest translators inherited from the Latin tradition the convention of philosophical and mythological glosses. They also exhibited a seemly inhibition in their strict adherence to prose throughout their versions. But translators like Bonaventura and Pierre merely imitated the outward form of the scholastic texts while resorting to their own popular resources for the medievalizing substance. Further decay of the academic format can be seen in those early mixed versions in which the glosses are selective and uncontroversial. As long as the *Consolatio* maintained its prestige in the schools against the encroachments of Aristotelianism, nominalism, and the contempt of familiarity, the production of vernacular versions formally reflected that reverence. But the Dominican and Benedictine religious who later romanced and refined the verse versions were exploiting the relaxation of academic conventions by certain kinds of poetic experimentation, unruffled by the intellectual storms higher up.

The quarter century that saw the verse elaboration of the *Consolatio* by the French Dominican Renaut de Louhans also witnessed the attack on the poetic theories of Albertino Mussato by the Dominican Giovanino of Mantua and the similar attack on Dante by the Dominican Guido Vernani of Rimini—an attack characterizing Dante as a "poetizing visionary and verbose sophist."[26] To understand Renaut's efforts in this hostile context

25. Siegfried Wenzel, "Chaucer's Troilus of Book IV," *PMLA* 79 (1964):542–547.
26. Ernst Curtius, *European Literature and the Latin Middle Ages,* trans. Willard Trask (New York, 1953), pp. 215–21.

we must glance at the nature of the famous Thomistic distruct of poetics. According to Ernst Curtius, St. Thomas Aquinas viewed poetry as the lowest of all sciences—his Aristotelian source being the *Metaphysics* and not the *Poetics*—and this was essentially a new view in opposition to the older northern rhetorical tradition embodied in the poetic epics of Bernard Silvester and Alain of Lille, and in the literary studies of John of Salisbury and William of Conches. The Dominicans were attacking, then, not poetry itself—recall Thomas's own great hymns—but the exalted place that theological poetics as a species of *scientia* had enjoyed in the high Latin tradition extending from Augustine and Boethius through Dante's vernacular union of poetry and philosophy.

Renaut's occasionally elaborate use of verse and his clear affection for *classica* is thus excused from liability to censure of the sort his fellow Dominicans directed at Dante and Mussato. It is possible to see, in consequence, a progressive weakening of the bonds between the two medieval cultures downward from Dante through the early Italian humanists and the English classicizers to the French translators, and this deterioration parallels the dissolution of that marriage of poetry and philosophy—successful in Dante—but on severe trial in the French adaptations of the *Consolatio*. The late classical union of philosophy and poetry achieved by Boethius was, as I have sketched, partly a formal matter of alternating the styles appropriate to prose and verse, partly an epistemological matter involving the quest for divine knowledge by both human reason, metaphorized as an ascent, and by Platonic reminiscence, made concrete through allusions to human and mythological history. Some of that allusiveness represents Boethius's admitted effort to hide his kernels from the vulgar, and scholastic allegorizing succeeded in discovering fruit only at the cost of multiplying chaff in the accumulation of troublesomely discordant narratives. Beyond this, the late medieval translators often lost the Boethian formal distinction by rendering the *Consolatio* entirely in prose or verse. And finally, some declined the interpreters' proffered nuts.

As nominalist theories moved late medieval philosophy away from allegorical and analogical modes toward a vision of the world as complex, ambiguous, and contingent,[27] so the translators' verse became extended narrative "digression," but some of the original outlines of the Boethian

---

27. Sheila Delany, "Undoing Substantial Connection: the Late Medieval Attack on Analogical Thought," *Mosaic* 5 (1972):31–52.

conjunction remain. In Dante the result is a series of dramatic narratives arrayed within an eschatological scheme; in the classicizing friars something of the same motivation produced pagan tales and *moralitates* set within explications of Holy Writ; while in certain of the French versions of Boethius the result is an attractive mixture of translation, gloss, and narrative elaboration.

In the texture of these French translations of the *Consolatio philosophiae* we can see an illustration of the essential eclecticism of medieval art and perhaps of the truth of Robert Jordan's suggestion that much of such art is *inorganic,* that it is significantly determined by its "exposed joints and seams, unresolved contradictions, and clashes of perspective."[28] If this is true, and I think it is, then we may be able to see in these translations, more easily perhaps than in the works of Chaucer, some of the aesthetic consequences, for better or worse, of that inorganicism. Here, I shall glance back at some of those results in terms of the failures and successes of the narratives as they extend or subvert Boethian meanings.

One of the structural effects of eclecticism results from drawing together several tellings of a story with much overlap of detail. This is neutral as regards meaning and may simply produce, as in the case of the relation of the Orpheus legend in the earliest prose translation, a mechanically repetitive account. But two of the narratives by the Anonymous of Meun realize two aesthetic possibilities of inorganic structure. The first of these successes is also partly owing to the shrinking interest among vernacular writers in the allegorical lucubrations of the schoolmen. Because he could discard much of the allegorizing that accompanied the narrative details gleaned from Fulgentius, Vincent of Beauvais, and the glosses, the Anonymous of Meun could also let those details fall in the direction of newer categories like the panorama of Deadly Sins. And the problematical redundancy of his account could be refined away by such revisions as that in MS B. N. fr. 1543. By associating Orpheus with *acedia* and Boethius with Orpheus, the Anonymous set the characterization of the Boethian malady of paralyzing ignorance within a rich medieval framework of greater accessibility.

A second positive aesthetic possibility also arose from the Anonymous's addiction to encyclopedias. And it bore fruit in his version of the

---

28. Robert M. Jordan, *Chaucer and the Shape of Creation: The Aesthetic Possibilities of Inorganic Structure* (Cambridge, Mass., 1967), p. 8.

tragedy of Croesus, where the result is not so much a medievalization of the Boethian notion of tragedy as a fuller exploitation of its nature than the original text allotted to exempla. The collection of reversals that the Anonymous assembled add up to a clear structural realization of the ideas that Fortune strikes with mechanical dispassion and that tragedy bewails such clockwork.

The tonal results of such inorganicism as we find exhibited in these translations appear to be even more mixed than those effected in structure. It must be granted, I think, that a number of the interpolated narratives, particularly those which were identified as pure fable—having little purpose beyond the merely informative—occasionally and inadvertently sabotaged the tone of their context. Partly this is due to the very limited range of tones permitted by the solemn purposes and lofty audience of the original *Consolatio,* but the apparent damage is also the result of the very freedom with which medieval authors assembled their bits and pieces into art.

When a translator intrudes into a hymn of universal love a rape story, he may impede our comprehension of universal love. But when he extends examples in a poem on death's universal sway to include more persons than Roman ex-consuls, he advances our understanding of the frightfulness of that sway. Between these extremes occur some interesting effects of medieval literary eclecticism.

I have claimed that the translators who reproduced the tendentious arguments of apologists for Christian cosmology shared their failure to significantly Christianize the *Consolatio.* But some translators were more successful in imparting a broadly Christian tone to the work. Thus, while Boethius certainly asserts the omnipotence of God, the vernacular adaptors extended the range of illustrations to include qualities of mercy and forgiveness in him. Similarly, the conception of human psychology that emerges from the interpolation of the homely instances that Pierre de Paris and Renaut de Louhans gathered of failed scholars and repentant thieves is more complex and more tolerant of complexity. Far from simply producing "unresolved contradictions," then, the extension of the meaning of the *Consolatio* that is accomplished through the accumulation of such narratives as we have examined is one of the Gothic glories of the inorganic methods of translators half a millenium ago. And while those methods may at times have cast an icon ungainly as a hawk in armor, more frequently they reflect the consolation His creatures have taken in the witty diversity of their imperfection.

Appendix I

Texts in Order of Discussion

I HAVE USED the following generally accepted principles for the transcription of Middle French texts: standard abbreviations have been silently expanded; punctuation, word-division, and capitalization are modern; *j* and *v* are used as consonants, *i* and *u* as vowels; use of accents and diaereses follows William Roach, *The Continuations of the Old French 'Perceval' of Chretien de Troyes,* vol. 1 (Philadelphia, 1949). The selections are the following:

1. Anonymous Burgundian on Calixto.
2. Renaut de Louhans on Croesus.
3. Anonymous of Meun on Croesus.
4. Anonymous Burgundian on Orpheus.
5. Anonymous of Meun on the Judgment of Paris.
6. Anonymous Benedictine's revision of Renaut de Louhans on Orpheus.
7. Renaut de Louhans's version of Book I, meter 2.
8. Anonymous Benedictine's version of Book I, meter 2.
9. Pierre de Paris on Alcibiades.
10. Anonymous Benedictine on the Inconstant Scholar.
11. Renaut de Louhans's stanzas on Death.

1. Anonymous Burgundian on Calixto. MS Vienna 2642, fol. 71–71v.

Calixto fu fille del roi Pandion. Jupiter l'ama por ce que bele esteit; bele boche aveit, e biau cors, e biau chief. Jupiter la preeit, e ele le despiseit, car ele voleit vivre caste ensemble Diana que esteit deesse de casteé. Par un jor Diana la mena chacier o sei e o sez autres compaignes e s'espandirent cea e la par le boiz chaceant. Jupiter esgarda del ciel e vit Calixto sole el boiz, laquele il aveit tant sovent proié. Il descendi as terres e prist la forme de Diana sa dame, e vint a li. Calixto le vit venir e cuida que fust sa dame, si se leva e ala encontre, si le salua. Jupiter li rendi sun salu dolcement e en riant, si l'embracea si la baisa, e la traist pres de sei e mostra li qu'il esteit Jupiter; car il jut a li, e ele conceut un enfant. Aprés long tens Diana conut e vit que ele esteit grosse, si la geta de sa compaignie. Calixto ot un enfant au tens que ot nom Arcas. Juno la femme de Jupiter conut le blasme de sun baron por l'enfant que fu nez; car por ce ne pot estre celer. Juno descendi a la terre e bati la damoisele durement, e si li dist: "Tu as esté molt bele, mais je te ferai molt laide." Isnelepas Juno la mua en orse, et quant ele fu muee, si s'en ala el bois o les autres bestes. Arcas li enfes crut e fu bachelier e alot sovent chacier. Par un jor il trova l'orse sa mere, e ne cuida pas que fust sa mere, e l'envaï ensemble l'espié. Jupiter l'esgarda e dist: "Ceste bataille n'est pas droituriere del fil e de la mere." Il les leva ambedous el ciel, s'en fist dous signes: li uns a nom la grantz orse, ce est li charz, li autres la petit orse. Juno conut ice qu'esteit feiz e fu molt plus dolente que devant, e dist: "Je lor cuida aveir mal fait, mais je lor ai bien feit. Je toli a la putain l'umeine [f. 71v] forme, ores est feite esteille en ciel." Juno s'en ala a Tetis, a la grant deesse de la mer, e a Oceanus sun baron, e si les proia que ne sofrissent que cist signes ne se plunjast en la mer. Il li otroierent. Por ce dïent li astrologien que li chars ne vait onques a dechaiement e ne se plunge en la mer come cez autres esteilles.

2.   Renaut de Louhans on Croesus.   MS B. N. fr. 578, fols. 14v–15.

Je croy bien que il te souvient
De Cressus qui fu roy de Lide,
Qui n'avoit pas la bourse vuide,
Ains riches et puissans estoit.
5   Le roy de Perse le doubtoit
Et avoit de lui grant paour
Pour sa richesse et sa valour.
Mais aprés, oultre une riviere,
Je changay toute ma maniere;
10   Car le roy de Perse le prist,
Par felonnie et par despit
Le mist en une grant fournaise.
Puis aprés li fis je tant d'aise,
Car une grant pluye du ciel vint

15 Qui toute la fournaise estint.
     Lors se commença a orguillier
     Quant il se dubt humilïer,
     Et s'esleva par vainne gloire;
     Ne retint pas en sa memoire
20 Comment je l'avoye tourné
     Et de bien en mal retourné.
     Et pour ce li fis je la moe,
     Car tost aprés tournay ma roe
     Qui n'a pas reposee longe,
25 Et li fis songer un tel songe:
     Une nuit li fut asemblant
     Qu'il estoit sur un arbre grant
     Ouquel Jupiter l'arrousoit
     Et Phebus aprés le sechoit.
30 Landemain quant il adjourna
     Ceste vision revela
     A une fille qu'il avoit
     Qui les secrez de dieu savoit.
     Quant elle oÿ la vision
35 Si fu en grant affliction,
     Car la fin vit qu'estoit amere.
     Si ne l'osa dire son pere
     Jusques ses peres l'en blasma;
     Lors en ceste guise parla   [fol. 15]
40 "Peres, voulez que je vous die
     Que vostre songe signiffie?
     L'arbre grant me fait crïer lasse,
     Car c'est la croix au roy de Perse,
     [Et le gibet qui est levez]
45 Ou vous serés mis et levéz.
     Jupiter vous arousera,
     Car la pluye vous moillera
     Qui descent de la region
     Ou il a fait sa mansion.
50 Phebus le souleil signifie
     Qui seche la chose moillie,
     Car aprés ce vous sechera

Que Jupiter vous moillera."
Ainsi advenir le couvient;
55 Un peu de temps aprés advient
Li roys de Perse le fist prendre
Et a son gibet le fist pendre.
C'est de ma roe la muance.
Aussi scez tu bien la mescheance
60 Qu'au roy de Perse vint aprés,
Car fut poursuiguz de si pres
Qu'il fut prins par la main d'un homme
Qu'estoit des conseilleurs de Romme
Qui par son nom avoit nom Paule;
65 Ne regarda palais ne saule,
Tresor, richesse, ne avoir
Que ne li feïsse savoir
De quel jeu jouer je sçay:
En jouer est toute ma joye.
70 Je le mis en si grant destroit
Celui qui si puissans estoit
Que cil qui l'avoit prins par armes
Plora forment a chaudes larmes
Quant il le vit en si mal point;
75 Ma roe de repos n'a point.

Selected variants: lines 14–16 Benedictine print has Du ciel luy vint une pluye grant /
Qui estaint la fournaise ardant / Lors commença a maistrier *and for lines 21–22* Puis
de mal en bien retourne / Pource luy donnay de ma poe *and it supplies line 44
missing from MS 578. In turn the print lacks line 51. MS B. N. fr. 812 has, in addition to the interpolation discussed in Ch. 2, added after line 33* Par la pourveance
divine / Qui tout scet et riens n'a devine. *For line 33, MS Roy. 20 A 19 has* Qui
exposer songes savoit.

3. Anonymous of Meun on Croesus. MS B. N. fr. 576, fols. 19–20v.

Comment es tu en ignorance
De nos moers? N'as tu ramembrance
Comment Cresus li roys de Lide
Ert resoingniés et ot accide
5 A Cyre Paule un roy de Perse;
Puis tantost par mescance adverse

Cyrus le prist et ordena
Qu'il fust ars, mais li cieuls donna
Pleuve que le fu estaindi,
10 Et Cresus de mort deffendi?
        Et pour fortune miex entendre
Voel mon parler plus loing estendre
De ces .ii. roys qui jadis furent,
Qui par long temps contens eürent.
15 Donc Cyrus avoit grant doubtance
De Cresus et de sa poissance,
Tant que Cyrus et les Persyens
Vinrent sur les Assirÿens.
Et fu lor terre desconfite
20 Par Cyrus et a lui subgite.
Donc Cresus si les vint secourre
Quant il ot les nouvelles courre,
Et s'enclot dedens Babilone
Comme ou cief dou regne et ou throsne
25 Dont Baltasar ert rois et sires
Encontre cui chevauchoit Cires.
Dont Cirus se traist celle part
S'a avironné sans depart
Babilone et du tout assise,
30 Tant qui l'eut par sa force prise
Et veés proëche de coer fiere.
        Babilone eut double riviere:
Gaugés qui au dehors l'enlace
Et Euffracés qui parmi passe.
35 Et a Gaugés en sen plus largue
Vint milles a droit mesurage,
Et est entour .C. piés parfons
Ou lieu ou il a plus bas fons,
Si com Marchÿanus tesmoingne
40 Qui escripst de celle besoingne.
Lucans en parole aultrement
Et dist que singulerement
Gaugés a son cours et sa voie
Contre orÿent, combien qu'on voie

45   Des aultres fleuves le contraire,
      Vers occident et ailleurs traire.
      Mais Solinus dist de ce fleuve
      Que les anguilles qu'on y treuve
      Ont communaument par nature
50   Entour .xxx. piés de mesure.
      Et s'estoit sus ce fleuve mis
      Cyrus contre ses anemis,
      Lors eut .i. chevalier vaillant
      Hardi, preu du corps assaillant
55   Qui sceut et vit le volenté
      Que li roys ot de la cité,
      Et fiert cheval des esporons
      En Gaugés, mais point n'esperons
      Qu'il n'i noyast, dont fu damages
60   Qui tousjours vient ou est outrages.
         Lors veïssiés Cyrus le roy,
      Et tout son ost en tel desroy,
      De courtois tristece et de ploer
      Qu'onques roys ne fist tel doleur,
65   Et jura qu'il prendroit la guerre   [fol. 19v]
      A le riviere et a son erre,
      Et la tourneroit en tel guise
      Qu'elle seroit sy a sec mise
      C'une femme le passeroit
70   Tout a piet et sy n'averoit
      Que jusques au genoul de l'iauwe.
      Ensi feroit sechier celle yauwe,
      Ensi jura, ensi le fist;
      En .xiiii. lieus deffist
75   Les rives tout parmi l'annee.
      Dont fu l'iauwe si escoulee
      Qu'il acompli tout son corage
      Qu'il avoit juré del passage.
         Et si come il fist de Gaugés,
80   Ensi fist faire d'Euffratés,
      Qui est de Gaugés trop plus grans;
      Car il estoit caus et engrans

Le mort son chevalier vengier
Et Babilone conquerir,
85 La plus noble cité du monde,
Tant qu'il enclot a le reonde.
Xvi. mille pas de mesure
Avoit pour cascune quarrure,
Qui font .lxiiii. mille
90 En .iiii. quartiers de la ville.
Et qui les pas voelt deviser
En piés pour le cerne viser,
Quatre .C. mille piés y troeve
Sicom geometrie proeve.
95 Des fortereches et des tours,
Et des tresgrans riches destours,
Des ydoles d'or et d'argent,
Des nobleces en peuple et en gent,
Et des autres biens qu'on y nombre
100 Nulle cités n'i fait fors umbre.
  La estoit li tours de Babel,
Donjon n'ot au monde si bel;
Xviii. mil piés estoit haulte.
Et la fu prise li deffaute
105 D'entendre le premier langage
Pour le grant orguel et l'outrage
Que Diex vit es enfans Noë
Que il avoit jadis loë.
Et en fist d'un .lx. et .x.
110 Dont point n'entendoient leurs dis,
Et se partirent de la tour
Et trairent cascuns a son atour.
  Et avoit Balthasar mil princes
Assamblés parmi ses provinces,
115 Roys, amiraus, et gent commune,
Sans l'autre gent d'armes menue
C'on ne poet savoir ne nombrer
Qui trop ne s'en voelt encombrer;
Et faisoient feste et grant joie
120 En delices ou raisons noie

De boire, d'estre aise, et mengier.
　　Mes Diex, qui se vault d'iaus vengier
Quant il les vit mengier et boire
Es vaissiaus—dont nous dist l'istoire
125　Que roys Nabugodnosor
Ot apporté en son tresor
De Jherusalem et du temple—
Leur monstra en loere un example
D'une merveilleuse aventure;
130　Car devant tous vint li joincture
D'un doit sans main et prist a poindre
Lettres et en ordene conjoindre,
Tant que .iii. mos ou mur escripst.
Mais nuls ne sceut lire l'escripst,
135　Tant que Danïel vint en place
Et dist au roy en mi sa face,
En presence de son conseil,
L'escripst: Mane, Pharés, Thecel.
Puis l'en dist l'exposition
140　Qui ert a sa confusion
Et li dist: "Rois, 'Mane' vault nombre　　[fol. 20]
Li premiers mos dont Diex te nombre
L'estat de ton poïr et ton regne,
Si t'en a ostee la regne.
145　　　"Li seconds mos a nom 'Pharés'
Car tu, morteuls et nonparés
A Dieu, qui riens mortel ne samble.
T'iés parés des vaissiaus du temple,
Et as l'onneur Dieu violee
150　En usant de cose sacree,
Dont 'Pharés' de Dieu te devise,
Que ta gloire est a honte mise.
　　　"Li tiers mos dist de ta sentence,
'Techel' que mis es en balance,
155　Et te troeve on en pechiés mainls
Et en vices et en biens vains,
Dont sans respit et sans remede
Cyrus roys de Perse et de Mede

Prendra Babilone ains demain
160 Et si t'ocira de sa main."
     Tost aprés vint li jours sans faille.
Cyrus apresta sa bataille,
Et passerent par la riviere
Gaugés sans moullier estriviere,
165 Puis sont en Euffratés venus,
L'autre fleuve, et se sont tenus
En chevauchant en leur eschielle,
Tant que sans assaut et eschielle
Se sont en Babilone mis,
170 Et ont pris tous leur anemis.
Et fuia Balthasar sa feste,
Car Cyrus li copa la teste,
Par arches qui estoient faites
Ou mur ou passoit li Euffratés.
175   Lors quant Cresus li rois de Lide,
Qui Balthasar faisoit aide,
Vit le meschief et le besoingne
Tantost de bien fuir s'ensoingne;
Ensy fuit com preus et hardis
180 Jusqu'a la cité de Sardis.
Mais Cyrus un petit sejourne
Et aprés sa bataille atourne,
Et prist tantost par sa proëche
Cresus dedens la fortereche.
185   Mais li fils de Cresus, Achis,
Muyans son temps, s'est aathis
De parler, qu'onques n'avoit fait
Par le plaisir Dieu qui tout fait,
Et crïa a vois eslevee:
190   "Cyrus, fortune tresmüee,
Com tu vois, et mi et mon pere
De prosperitet en misere,
T'argüe pour nous et te somme,
Que tu te congnoisces pour homme
195 A qui il poet mesavenir,
Si com tu nous vois avenir.

               Dont raisons te doit esmouvoir
               A pitet de nos mauls avoir.”
               Lors quant Cyrus ot teil merveille
200   Et comment misere pareille
               Li poet venir se si acorde,
               Et tantost a yauls se racorde
               Sauvé leur vie et leurs biens tous,
               Car pitieus ert, non pas estous.
205   Mais aprés celle grace belle
               Fist Cresus traïson nouvelle
               Contre Cyrus, et esmut guerre
               Pour fouler son regne et sa terre,
               Et avint qu’il eürent bataille.
210   Mais justice qui a droit taille
               Paya son orguel sans demoere,
               Et le prist Cyrus eus en loere;
               Et puis fist .i. feu aprester,
               Et Cresus enmi lieu getter,
215   Et l’eüst ars, se fortune noeuve
               N’eüst fait descendre si grant pleuve
               Que tous li feus en fu estains,   [fol. 20v]
               Ains qu’il fust de la forche attains,
               Dont Cresus fu ensi delivres,
220   Si com dist l’ystoire et li livres.
               Quar cascuns se retraist arriere
               Pour la grant pleuve et la fumiere;
               Et Cresus s’en fuit aultre voie
               Quant on cuide qu’il se fourvoie
225   En la pleuve et en la fournaise.
               Mais Fortune tout sans mesaise
               Le delivre de le main Cyre.
                   Dont il malvais encore empire;
               Et pensa li malvais Cresus
230   Qu’encor courroit il Cyre sus
               A sa grant meschance darraine,
               Si com par vision certaine
               Li fu monstré en son songant
               Qu’il se veoit hault sus la gent.
235   Et si veoit son dieu, Jovis,

Arouser son chief et son vis
De l'arousee du ciel doulce,
Et puis le soleil qui tout ce
Essvoit, et si le seschyeve.
240 Au matin a l'oere qu'il lieve
Et s'est de ce mult merveilliés
Quant du songe s'est esveilliés,
Et vint a Phania sa fille,
Une clergesse mult soubtille,
245 Et li a sa vision dite.
Et elle li expose triste
La vision et la sentence:
    "Biaus peres, pechiés qui t'enpence
D'orguel et d'outrecuiderie
250 Te doit briefment tollir la vie,
Pour ce que tu n'as ramembrance
Jadis de ta double mescance;
Comment Cyrus te desconfit,
Et des graces que Diex te fit
255 Sauver ta vie et le tien rendre.
Et si voels de nouvel emprendre
Contre Cyrus et rebeller,
Dont Diex t'a volut monstrer
L'issue qui t'en avenra;
260 Car Cyrus encor te prendra
Et dessus la gent en la cruis
Te prendera si com je truis.
Aprés arousera ton cief
Et ton vis Jovis de rechief;
265 Soleil fera ta fache sesche,
Osy com Jovis l'ot fait fresche."
    Ensi en fu com Phania
Sa fille demonstré ly a,
Car puis eut a Cyre un conflit
270 Ou bleciet le prist et afflit,
Et le fist haut en la crois mettre
Pour le prophetise vraye estre.
Ensi ly a Fortune amere
Cangiet tous biens en grant misere.

4. Anonymous Burgundian on Orpheus. MS Vienna 2642, fols. 51v–54.

Cil est bieneürez qui pot veeir la clere funtaine de bien. Cil est beneürez qui se pot deslïer des lïens de la pesant terre. Uns poëtes de Trace de
cele terre, qui aveit nom Orpheüs, plora jadis la mort de sa femme. Il fist
les selves moveir e corre a sei par ses plorables chanz, e constreinst les
[fol. 52] aigues ester, e li cers ajosta sun costé neient dotable ensemble les
crüels lions, e li lievres ne dota le veu chien, quar li chiens esteit apaisiez
por le dolz chant. L'amor eschaufantz constreigneit le cuer d'Orpheï
dedenz. Li chant li quel aveient vencu cez autres choses ne poënt asuagier
lor seignor, e il complaignantz de la durece des dex sovereins requist les
enfernaus maisons. Il atempra iloec les soëfs chans par les cordes bien
sonantz, e il chanta en plorant queque chose il aveit espuisé des meillors
fonteines de la deesse sa mere; ce est, il chantot au mielz qu'il saveit. E il
chante ce que li plors molt poissantz li amonesteit, e l'amors doblantz le
plor. Les valees d'enfer sunt commovés par le douz chant. Orpheüs prie
pardon par dolce proiere as seignors des armes. Li portiers d'enfer, qui
aveit a nom Cerberus e aveit treis testes, se merveille del novel chant e fu
esbaïz. Les treis deesses serors, Megera, Alleto, Tesiphone, vengerresses des
felonies les quels demeinent les armes noissantz par paor, e eles tristes ja
emmostissent de lermes.

L'isnele roe ne trebuche Ixion cel geiant, e Tantalus, destruitz par
longe sei[f], despit les aigues. Li voltors, quant il est saols par les chantz,
ne depecea la gole de Ticii, del geiant. Le jugieres des armes en ot pitié a la
parfin, e dist, "Vencu somes; nos donons au baron sa femme que il a
achetee par sun chant, mais une leis estrecera les dons, que il n'en ait
licence de flechir arriere ses iouz tant que il seit fors d'enfer." Qui puisse
doner aucune lei as amantz? Nuls ne le poet doner. Amors est la plus
grantz leis a sei. Ce est, amors est senz lei. Amors a lei estre senz lei. Heu
las, Orpheüs vit la soe Euridicem (issi aveit nom sa femme) pres de le issue
de la nuit, ce est del oscur enfer. Il la vit, si la perdi, ele chaï arriere.

La glose de cest metre: Nos devons saveir que li demonstrementz des
auctors e des philosofes est feite par treis manieres: par fables, o par
estoires, o par integument. Fable si est chose feinte semblant de veir, ausi
come fait Ovides. Hystoire si est chose feite recontee [fol. 52v] issi comme
ele fu feite. Integumentz est quant om dit une chose e senefie autre, si
come est ici de Orpheo. Ce apele hom en divinité allegorie. Ce est la fable
de Orpheo.

Orpheüs fu uns poetes de Trace de cele contree, e saveit molt bien harper. It aveit une femme qui aveit a nom Euridice. Ele esteit molt bele e delitable. Aristeüs uns riche pastor l'ama e ele le despiseit, e fuiet par les prez nuz piez, e Aristeüs la sigueit, e ele tocha a un serpent. Li serpentz la morst, e ele fu morte. Orpheüs conut la mort de sa femme, e fist grantz plaignementz, e comencea a chanter o sa harpe por sei conforter. Il fist les arbres corre aprés sei par sun douz chant, e constreinst les aigues ester. Li cers aleit segurement ensemble le lion. Li lievres n'en ot paor del chien, quar il esteit en paiz por le chant. L'amors de sa femme plus eschaufantz li embrasot le cuer dedenz. Por ce li chant liquel aveient vencu cez autres choses ne pöeient assoagier lor seignor. Il se compleinst des damnedeus desus, e descendi en enfer. Iloec comencea a chanter au mielz que il sot e pot, e vint devant le seignor des armes, e si li dist: "Je ne sui pas ci venuz por batre tun portier come fist Hercules. Je i sui venuz por ma femme, que est morte novelement. Sa amor me constreinst que je sofrisse cest grant travaill por li raveïr, e je vos pri, rendez la mei." Il chanteit tote voies molt dolcement. Les armes comencerent a plorer por le dolz chant. Li tres maistre deable d'enfer, ce sunt les treis serors, commencerent premiere- ment a plorer.

Li torment de Ixyon de la roe cessa. Yxion fu uns geiante qui apela Junone, la femme de Jupiter, de gesir od sei, e por ce il a tel poine en enfer que il est torneez en une roe. Or disoms l'entegument de ce. Par Junonem devoms entendre la vie temporel. Par Yxion, qui vost gesir o Junone e qui est tornoiez en la roe, devoms entendre celui qui quiert delit as temporels choses, mais ne poet venir a fin.

Tantalus n'ot cure de mangier ne de beivre por le chant. Tan- [fol. 53] talus fu uns usuriers e despiseit Pallas, cele deesse de sapience. Il sofreit tel poine en enfer: il a faim, e a une pome vermoille pendue devant sei; quant il la viout prendre, ele fuit ariere. Il a seif; l'aigue li est au mentun e ne poet beivre. L'entegument est itel: par Pallas devons entendre la vie con- templative, ce est l'espiritel. Par Tantalus qui despist Pallas entendoms les usuriers qui despisent la sapience spiritel. Il veeient la pome e n'en poeent mangier, e l'aigue e n'en poeent beivre, come Tantalus, quar il ont les richesces temporels, e n'en poënt estre saole.

Li voltors ne traist la gole de Ticii por les douz chanz. Ticius, selong la fable, volst gesir ensemble Venus qui esteit molt bele femme e deesse d'amor. Il a tel torment en enfer, quar li voltor li manjüent la gole tote la semaine josqu'al samedi, e au lundi est toz entiers. L'entegument ist itel: Venus est deesse de delit. Par Ticius devoms entendre cez qui desirent le delit de luxure. Par les voltors qui lor manjüent les goles, devoms entendre les vices qui commovent la volenté des homes a la luxure, quar en la gole est li apetites e li desiriers des homes. Parce que au lundi recreist la gole entendoms quant plus usoms la luxure tant creist plus e plus enforcé.

Li sires d'enfer ot pitié de Orpheüs, e li rendi sa femme par tel covenant que il ne gardast derriere sei tant que il fust fors d'enfer. A bien pres Orpheüs esteit ja fors ensemble sa moillier, il esgarda derriere, si la vit, si la perdi. Iceste fable regarde a vos, o vos homme, quicunques volez mener vostre pensé en la sovereine lumiere, ce est en Deu. Quar cil liquels vencuz flechira ses lumieres, ce est, reison e entendement, en l'enfernal fosse, il perdra quanque il aveit de bien dementres que il esgarde les enfernals choses. De ce meesme dit l'Evangile, "Cil qui met sa main en la charrue e esgarde arriere, non est dignes del regne de Deu." Ce est, [fol. 53v] quant li hom commence le bien, ne deit retorner au mal.

Or diroms l'entegument de Orpheüs. Orpheüs dit autant cumme voiz d'or. Il fu poëtes, ce est sages, e saveit molt bien harper, ce est raisnablement saveit parler, Cil est perfeitement sages qui a sapience e eloquence. Car Tulles dit el prologue de retorique, "Eloquence senz sapience nu ist. Sapience senz eloquence petit parfite, car ele est come li tresors resconduz e li arcs que non est tenduz." Orpheüs ot une femme que ot nom Euridice. Euridice ce est bien disantz. Ele esteit bele e delitable, ce est, qui bien dit, si est de bones murs e delitables e amiables. Par Euridicem devoms entendre la natural coveitié. Naturals coveitié si est mangiers e beivre e les naturels autres choses. Ou par Euridice pooms entendre la sapience del sages.

Aristeüs uns riches pastor l'ama. Ares en grezeis, ce est vertus en romans. Theos, ce est Dex. Por ce disoms Aristeüs vertu de Deu. La vertu de Deu deit mener e guïer nostre naturel coveitié ou nostre sapience. Aristeüs ama Euridicem, ce est, la vertuz de Deu aime la natural coveitié, e la viout traire vers sei. Mais ele fuit par les prez, ce est, par les delitz del siecle. Li serpentz la morst el pié, ce est, li deables l'engine e la meine malvaise voie. Ele muert, ce est, ele porrist en sun pechié.

Orpheüs conut la mort de sa moillier e fist grantz plaignementz. Ce est, li sages est corrociez quant la naturel coveitié gist en pechié. Il chanteit dolcement par sa harpe por sei conforter, ce est, il diseit dolces paroles e raisnables. Les selves coreient aprés lui, ce est, li home fol e neient enseigné le sigueent por ses dolces paroles e raisnables. Orpheüs faseit les aigues corrantz ester, quar li sages fait les homes qui sunt movant cum aigue estre estables. Li cers alot ensemble le lion, ce est, li fous e li coardz vait par l'atemprement del sage ensemble le sage e le hardi. Li lievres ne doteit neient le chien. Ce est, li feibles ne doteit neient le fort, car li fortz esteit atemprez par les dolces paroles. Quant Orpheüs vit que ne se poet conforter, laissa les souveraines choses e descendi en enfer por raveïr sa moillier, ce [fol. 54] est, li sages converse a la fiee d'environ les temporels choses que il poisse retraire le natural coveitié as celestials choses.

Orpheüs chanta iloec molt dolcement, e les treis serors d'enfer plorerent por la dolceor del chant. Ce senefie que li sages parole reisnablement des temporels choses. Par les treis serors que plorerent devoms entendre que nos pechoms en treis manieres en cest siecle, que nos entendoms par enfer: en penser, en dit, e en fait. Quant li sages hom parole, cez treis serors deivent plorer e repentir. Le reis e la reine d'enfer, vencu par la dolceor del chant, rendirent a Orpheüs sa femme par tel covenant que il ne regardast derriere sei. Par le rei e la reine d'enfer devoms entendre reison e entendement que sunt goveneor de cest siecle. Car raisons e entendement rameinent la natural coveitié as celestiaus choses par les raisnables paroles del sage. Orpheüs regarda derriere e vit sa femme, si la perdi. Sovent avient que li sages aime trop natural coveitié, e la regarde derriere, ce est, a mal e si la pert. Orpheüs s'en torna desus. En aprés grant tens la proueresse de Bachi, del deu del vin, l'ocistrent. Ce est, que sovent avient que li sages hom pert por le vin qu'il a beu oltre mesure les .v. sens: le veeir, l'oïr, le goster, le flairer, le tochier, e est ausi come mortz. De ce dit Salemons, "Li vins e les femmes font meesmes les sagese foleer."

5. Anonymous of Meun on the Judgment of Paris. MS B. N. fr. 576, fols. 51v–52v.

Mais pour solas un petit faire
Voel de .iii. dieuesses retraire,
Dont poëtes font mention,
Quant attient a m'entention:
5 Juno, Pallas, l'autre Venus,
Par qui moult de mauls sont venus.
Juno si vault le vie active,
Et Pallas la contemplative,
Et Venus emporte delit
10 Que cascuns a bien pres eslit.

Juno dont li vie active
Donne rikece et signourie,
Et se tient un septre en se main,
Car regner fait desir humain;
15 Et a en se garde un pavon,
Car on l'aime et se le loe on
Pour les vestimens curieuls
Qu'ont li riche delicieus;
Et est a Hercules marastre,
20 Car empeechier voelt et debatre
Vie active, Hercules le sage
Science avoir en amistage.
    Mais Pallas donne sapience
De dieu et de sa congnoissance.
25   Et Venus, li dame amoureuse,
Est de delis tres savoureuse,
Meismement en delis de femme
Qui les amans art et enflamme.
Avoec ly se va cils couchier,
30 Cui convoitise poet touchier
D'onneur mondaine et de haultece
Faire se fin et se dieuesse;
Mais n'est que nue et se fourerre
Et sa semence chiet en terre.
35 Dont il engingnier Juno cuide
Qui li escape toute voide,
Et chiet en terre s'engenreure,
Dont gayant de double nature,
Moytiet homme moitiet cheval,
40 Sont né sans raison a travail;
Car cil homme si sont com bestes
Qui de ce monde font leur festes,
Et tousjours sont tourné en roe,
Car li mondes tousjours se mue.
45   Mais quant a ore m'en delivre,
Car dit en ay ou premier livre
Qui fu Venus et de quel pere,
Et comment est li noms se mere.

Si voel chi dire une merveille
50 Qui des aultres .ii. despereille,
Juno riche, Pallas la sage,
Venus la douche en amistage.   [fol. 52]
Car jadis par une estrivee
Ces .iii. dames eürent meslee,
55 Et contentions fors et grans,
En ce que cascune ert engrans
De l'une a l'autre comparer,
Et que mielx se pooit on parer
De s'amour et de sa bargaingne,
60 Qu'on ne fesist de sa compaigne.
Et estoit leur rihotte celle
Que cascune estoit li plus belle;
Et pour estre certefyés
Sont a Jupiter adreciés,
65 Et l'ont pris pour arbitre et juge
Que il la verité en juge.
Mais li diex si n'en volt jugier,
Ains on a commis le jugier
Au fil le roy Priant, Paris,
70 Qui puis fu Helaine maris,
Si com je le propose a mettre
Ou quart livre et ou darrain metre.
Dont li diex si lor a jettee
Une pomme d'or et lettree
75 En .ii. filles soubtieuls escrois:
"Je sui le plus belle des trois."
Donc quant Paris eut veut le pomme,
Trop li fu fais et a somme
Li jugiers, et fu tous pensus
80 Qui d'elles .iii. belle estoit plus.
      Mais Juno vers Paris s'avanche:
"Voels avoir royaume et chevanche?
Je t'en feray parfaites donnes,
Se tu le pomme d'or me donnes.
85 Et te donray quanques habonde
De richece et d'avoir ou monde."

>   Et dist Pallas, "Ce n'est nïant
>   Juno, tu le vas faunïant
>   En donnant richece et avoir.
> 90   Mais je, li dame de savoir,
>   Li feray savoir que c'est diex,
>   Et se li monsterray as yex
>   Comment toute cose en decline
>   Com de sa cause, et si rencline
> 95   A son retour et a se fin,
>   Com a se bonneureuse fin,
>   Quel cose c'est dou firmament,
>   De ses cours, de leur mouvement,
>   Et en aprés des .vii. planettes
> 100   De leur erres et de leur mettes,
>   Des elemens, des creatures
>   Qui en sont en mainltes faitures,
>   Des angles ossy, et des ames
>   Que tu point ne cognois ne ames.
> 105   Com on doit vivre en bonnes moers;
>   Qui ne scet li mondes poy meurs.
>   Dont en ce que li habandonne,
>   Trop plus grand don de ty li donne,
>   Car savoirs l'omme adourne et pere
> 110   Ne nulle riens ne si compere;
>   Ains est boe ordure et viltés,
>   Et menchonnable vanités
>   Toute richece temporee
>   A sapience comparee,
> 115   Si com le conclut par raison
>   Cil qui les eut en sa maison,
>   Salemons en ces .ii. contens
>   Sour tous les hommes de son temps.
>   Dont la pomme me doit donner
> 120   Cui sy en voel guerredonner."
>   Quant Venus oÿ les paroles,
>   Si les tint toutes .ii. pour folles;
>   Puis commenche .i. doulcet a rire
>   A Paris et li prist a dire

125 Qu'elles le tenoient de truffes,
   Plaines de ruses et de buffes,
   Mais elle li donroit tel don
   Qu'il n'aroit point de guerredon.   [fol. 52v]
   Et qu'on ne porroit desservir
130 S'il le voloit sans plus servir,
   Que le pomme d'or peust avoir,
   Car miex vault sour tout aultre avoir
   De Juno et dou sens Pallas
   Joie d'amours et de sollas,
135 D'amant vray et d'amie ensamble
   C'uns coers et vus volloirs assamble;
   Ne n'est riens qu'on plus rouver doie
   Quand on a de ses amours joie.
   "Et je," dist elle, "suy maistresse
140 Des delis d'amours et dieuesse,
   Et si sont par moy departis
   A ceuls qu'avoec moy sench partis.
   Et pour tant, Paris, je te part
   Que se tu te tiens en ma part
145 Contre ces .ii. dames premieres,
   Qui ne te sont que losengieres,
   Je t'ay une femme pourveue
   Qu'onques plus belle ne fu veue
   Pour deliter et solacyer
150 En s'amour et son embracier,
   Se tu le pomme d'or m'otroies.
   Et pour voir se tu le me noies
   Tu as tous mes delis perdus."
   Lors Paris trestous esperdus
155 Et souspris des parlers Venus,
   En est par devers li venus,
   Et s'est devant ses piés jettés,
   A tous ses voloirs aprestés,
   Et dist: "Dame, vescy le pomme,
160 Je le vous doins; et moy, vostre homme,
   Voelliés rechevoir en hommage
   En vostre savoureus mainnage.

> Je le vous doins, doulce pucelle,
> Pour le milleur et le plus belle."
165 Ensi a Paris terminee
> Leur tenchon et leur estrivee,
> Et encor avient il souvent
> Que les biens que diex a couvent,
> Et li mondes sont desprisiés,
170 Pour les dars Venus agguisiés.

*The following are the major deletions and revisions of this section to be found in MS
B. N. fr. 1543. Deleted passages: lines 23–28; 61–63; 71–72; 85–86; 111–114. Re-
written passages: for lines 35–44 read:*

> Et tout ainsi comme exposee
> Est dessus soit chi demenee
> De Juno toute la samblance
> A parler de parler manance,
> Car Pallas sapience donne
> De dieu et cognissance bonne.
> Et Venus, la dame amoureuse,
> Et sus toutes delicïeuse
> Meïsment en deduit de fame
> Que les amans art et enflamme.

For lines 64–69 read

> Si ont a Jupiter commis
> Qu'il en juge, mais il a mis
> Le content de tout sur Paris,
> Qui fu a Helaine maris,
> Et fieuls au roy de Troies, Priant,
> Que de jugier vont si priant.

For lines 97–106 read Et toute autre cose congnoistre / Qui peut cree et faite estre.
For lines 127–150 read:

> Et dit "Paris, se tu me fois le don
> De la pomme pour guerredon,
> Te donray d'amour le solas
> Qui mieuls vault que le dons Pallas,
> Ne Juno, car en ceste vie
> N'a bien que joyr de s'amie.

And for lines 161–164 read Car a la plus belle vous tieng / Recheves me en vostre
maintieng.

6. Anonymous Benedictine's revision of Renaut de Louhans on Orpheus. Print [Geneva: Jean Croquet, before 1481], sig. g2–g3v.

Bien heüreux seroit pour voir
Cil qui la fontaine vëoir
Pourroit bien de verité pure.
Bien heüree est creature
5 Qui les lieux de terre obscure
Peult deslier par pensee pure.   [sig. g2v]
Orpheüs fut sa en arriere
Ung menestrier de grant maniere
Qui fasoit chant moult delitables,
10 Selonce que dient les fables,
Et fut souverains musiciens
Et bien touchoit les instrumens,
Et fut nez et nourry en Trece
En une partie de Grece.
15 Une tresdoulce amie avoit
Que Erudice on nommoit.
Advint qui perdit celle amie,
Dont moult mena doulente vie;
Car long temps luy courrut aprés
20 Par boys, par champs, et par pres,
Toutesvoyes en complaingnant,
Tousjours aloit chalemelant
Les doulceurs de ses chalemeaux.
Les chasnes et les grans ormeaux
25 Faisoit troter et courre en dance.
Les rivieres qui par pesance
Encontre le val fort courroient
A son tresdoulx chant s'arrestoient;
Le cerf se joingnoit au lÿon,
30 Et le lievre au chien felon
Pour sa tresdoulce melodie
Qu'il faisoit en querant s'amie.
Quant ne la peult trouver sur terre,
En enfer la voult aler querre,

35   Et se complaint des dieux d'amont
       Qui de ses pleurs semblant ne font,
       Car ne luy veulent reveler
       Ou s'amie pourra trouver.
       Quant il voult en enfer descendre
40   Ses instrumens forment fist tendre,
       Si que n'y eut clef ne müance
       Qui ne fust selon l'accordance.
       Calÿope, qui le chant fist
       Et qui tout son chant luy aprist,
45   Grant desire ha de tel chant faire
       Qui aux dieux d'enfer puisse plaire.
       Chant ne le povoit conforter,
       Amour faisoit son plour doubter.
       Graces prioit aux dieux umbrages,
50   Et si leur faisoit grans hommages
       Quant Orpheüs vient a la porte
       D'enfer; adonc se desconforte,
       Car a la porte ung chien demeure
       Qui tout derompt et tout deveure,
55   Que l'on appelle Cerberus.
       Lors fut esbahy Orpheüs,
       Car ce matin havoit trois testes,
       Ce que n'ont pas les aultres bestes.
       Si print a touchier sa vïelle
60   Si doulcement qu'a sa cordelle
       Attrait le matin deputaire,
       Et la fait doulx et debonnaire.
       Quant il eut le portier passé,
       Qui ne l'eut ne mort ne cassé,
65   Si encontra les troys deesses
       Qui sont encor plus felonesses;
       En cest siecle les ames temptent
       Et en l'autre, fort les tormentent.
       Quant regarda ces forsennees
70   Ne fut pas seur de ses denrees,
       Et non pourtant avant ala,
       Et si doulcement vïela

Qu'il fist au doulx son de sa corde
Encliner a misericorde   [sig. g3]
75 Celles qui tormentent les ames,
Et leur font getter maintes larmes.
Quant Orpheüs eut eschappé
Les dyablesses et passé,
Si trouva la roe Yssion
80 Tournant a grant affliction.
Yssion fut pour ses pechiés
En une grant roe attachiés
Par piés, par mains, et par teste.
Celle roe point ne s'arreste;
85 Repos n'a que tousjours ne torne,
Car de jour et de nuyt retorne.
Orpheüs print si doulcement
A demener son instrument,
Que pour son tresdoulx violer
90 La roe cesse a roëler,
Aussi com celle eüst envie
D'entendre celle melodie.
Aussi se porta Orpheüs
Moult bien par devers Tantalus.
95 Tantalus en une saison
Les dieux semont en sa maison,
Et fist grant mangier et grant feste,
Mais en fin luy vint moleste,
Car quant voit que luy fault vitaille
100 Son propre filz par morseaux taille,
Et le met cuyre pour mangier.
Les dieux doivent tout ce vangier;
De ce crime garde se prindrent,
Et durement ilz le pugnirent,
105 Car Tantalus est condempnez
En enfer avec les dampnez,
Ou il est en une riviere
Si plongiés devant et derrirre
Que o le menton l'eaue touche,
110 Et si n'en peult mettre en sa bouche.

Ains quant il voit l'onde venir,
Et il la cuyde retenir,
L'onde tantost arriere fuyt;
Ainsi meurt de soif jour et nuyt.
115 Ung grant pommier est en la place
Qui son fruict luy met en sa face.
Quant il cuyde la pomme mordre,
Elle ne fait que soy estordre,
A l'autre part prent a voler:
120 Pour ce ne la peult engouler;
Ainsi meurt de soif et de fain,
Cil qui vitaille ha en la main.
Quant Tantalus ouyt la note
Qui par bemol fut moult devote,
125 Tant fut sourpris et esbahys
Et en joye de cueur ravis
Que la fain et la soif oublie
En escoutant la melodie.
Tucius estoit d'aultrepart
130 Qui fut homme de male part,
Qui par sa grant transgression
Est en moult grant affliction;
Car ung voultour, oysel de proye,
De son ventre luy tolt le foye.
135 Quant le voultour ouy le chant,
Qui melodie causoit grant,
Pour la doulceur lieve la teste
Et du mangier tantost s'arreste.
Or s'en va Orpheüs sa voye
140 En plourant fait semblant de joye,
Mais de grant joye n'y a point
Car l'aguillon d'amour le point.   [sig. g3v]
Au roy d'enfer c'est arresté,
Comme dolent et courroucié.
145 Aulcunefois le corde touche,
Aulcunefois chante de bouche,
Soit par bouche ou touche de corde
Tousjours requiert misericorde,

Et en chantant grace supplie.
150 Que voulez vous que je vous die?
Tant a viellé et chanté
Qu'il ha les diables enchanté.
Le roy d'enfer tantost s'accorde
C'on lui face misericorde.
155 "Rendons," dist il, "cestui s'amie,
Car par chanter la bien gaingnie,
Mais tant lui mettons nous de loy
Qu'il ne regarde derrier soy
Jusques a tant qu'il ait menee
160 Oultre toute nostre contré."
Mais la loy d'amour est si fort
Qu'elle crainct peine ne mort;
Dont cest fole peine et errour
De bailler loy a fine amour,
165 Car Orpheüs fut amans fins.
Quant d'enfer regarda les fins,
Son regard torne par derriere
Pour regarder s'amie chiere;
Et pour ce que la loy n'a tenue,
170 S'amie tantost a perdue:
En enfer va comme devant.
Ja fine la fable atant.
A vous recorde ceste fable
Qui querez le jour perdurable,
175 Et ja vous estes mis a voye.
Gardés vous bien que faulse joye
Ne vous puisse tourner arriere,
Et perdre ceste grant lumiere;
Qui bien veult en enfer penser
180 De tous maulx se doit bien tenser,
Ne pour ung tout seul deduit faire
Point ne doit son appetit traire,
En ce püant venimeux gouffre
Ou sans fin art l'eternal souffre.

The following readings from MS N. L. W. 5038 are to be preferred to those in the print: line 48 for doubter *read* doubler; *lines 57 and 61 for* matin *read* mastin; *line 89 for* violer *read* vieller; *line 180 for* tenser *read* cesser.

7. Renaut de Louhans's version of Book I, meter 2. MS B. N. fr. 578, fol. 3–3v.

Helas, com raison et lumiere
D'omme dechiet en grant maniere
Et devient troublé et obscure;
Celle qui premierement ere   [fol. 3v]
5 Faite de si noble matiere
Des biens mondains aprins la cure.
Certes c'est viltez et ordure
Quant si tresbelle creature
Se veult rester en la poussiere.
10 S'elle regardoit sa nature
Et la biauté de sa faiture,
Elle trairoit son pié arriere.

He, Fortune desmesuree,
Com as nature bestournee.
15 Par erreur et par ygnorance
Cilz home, qui toute sa pensee
A tousjours au ciel ordonnee
Pour avoir de lui cognoissance,
Est maintenant par ta muance
20 Entrez en si grant non-puissance
Que sa raison est enclinee.
Tu l'as mis en une balance
D'une part qui par sa pensance
Ne puet en hault estre eslevee.

25 Il cognoissoit souleil et lune
Oultre cognoissance commune,
Cours d'estoilles et de planettes,
Or a cognoissance si brune
Par la muance de Fortune
30 Qui ne cognoit ne cours ne mectes.
Helas, Fortune, quelz vous estes
Qu'avez mis ou nombre des bestes
Celui qu'avoit raison aucune?
Certes voz solas et voz festes

35 Sont souvent plainnes de molestes,
    Ja n'en seront long temps senz une.

    Cilz qui rendoit raison et cause
    De toute chose haulte et basse
    Maintenant a raison perdue.
40 Bien est Fortune fort et fausse
    Qui si fort armes fiert et fausse
    Quant de bien en mal se remue.
    Elle fait d'omme beste mue,
    Car tourner li fait sa veüe
45 A la terre qui tant est basse.
    La raison qu'estoit bien vestue
    De nostre habit fait toute nue.
    Pour ce me couvient crier 'lasse.'

    Lasse moy, ce n'est pas Boëce,
50 De grant vertu, de grant noblesse,
    Qui la fleur d'entendement porte;
    N'est pas cheüz en tel foiblesse
    Par desconfort ne par tristesse
    Cil qui tout autre reconforte.
55 Mais de ce dire me deporte,
    Raison est que je le supporte
    Quant il est entrez en vieillesse;
    Car souvent a ouvert ma porte
    Pour oïr ce que je enorte
60 Quant il estoit en sa jeunesse.

    Or aprins autrepart son erre.
    Je scey certainnement qu'il erre
    Quant il ne nous voit ne visite,
    Mais Fortune si fort l'enserre
65 Que tousjours a contre nous guerre,
    Que ne savons ou il habite.
    Fortune doit bien estre dicte,
    Car en forcener si delicte.
    Plus forcenant ne couvient querre

70   Un homme de treshault merite;
     Par forcenerie subite
     A tout encline vers la terre.

**8. Anonymous Benedictine's version of Book I, meter 2. Text is from MS
B. N. fr. 12459, but material added from Renaut has been deleted to illustrate stage one of the text. See discussion.**

     Helas, comme humain pensee
     Plaine de grant merancolie
     En parfonde fosse est boutee,
     Et sa propre clarté laisee
5   Toute en tenebreuse contré,
     Chargié d'ordure et de lie,
     Des biens terriens fors souflee,
     Sans fin croist sa merancolie.

     Cest homme Boëce jadis,   [fol. 4]
10   Qui en science moult habondoit,
     Plain de franchise ou ciel ravis,
     D'ouvrir le ciel coustume avoit;
     Et jugoit par commun avis,
     Et proprement determinoit
15   Du rouge soleil le pourpris,
     Car la verité bien savoit.

     Des estoilles et de leurs cours haultains,
     De lune et de sa froidure dittoit,
     Et comptoit par nombres certains,
20   Et les momens determinoit,
     Mais plus car il estoit certains,
     Et clerement le demonstroit,
     Dont viennent les vens si haultains
     Qui fort sufflent c'on les oÿt.

25   Et mesmement la mer serie,
     Aussi estoit ce s'estudie
     Que c'est qui muet le ciel estable;
     Parquoy l'estoille delittable,

Lucifer, aprés qu'est couchie
30 Dessus la mer en occident,
Puis au matin qu'est resveillie
Clere reluit en orient.

Aussie discerne il proprement
Qui cause en printemps le doulx vent,
35 Dont la terre est toute florie
Et aournee cointement
Des roses; aussi scet comment
Autompne la vigne chargie
De raisins donne plainement.
40 A brief parler finablement,
Cest homme si cautellement
Cognoist et scet par sa clergie
De la terre et du firmament
Tout le secret contenement.
45 Las, or voy comment est vuidie
Sa pensee d'entendement,
Et de chaines si durement
Est sa raison si enlacie,
Que contrains est hastivement
50 De regarder pitousement
Pour l'amour de sa maladie.

There are many variants in the MSS and the Croquet print; e.g. for line 20 read Les movemens des cours haultains; *for line 48 read* Est sa chiere si enchaiennee; *and for line 51 read* La terre de face esbahy. *Lines 52–83 closely follow the text of Renaut in MS B. N. fr. 578.*

9. **Pierre de Paris on Alcibiades.   MS Vat. lat. 4788, fol. 53v.**

Philosophie raconte en ceste part .i. estoyre, c'est assaver que une femme fu qui ot nom Alchïadis, et fu moult belle. Car elle passoit a son vivant toutes femes de biauté, et estoit cele Alchïadis amie de Alixandre. Si avint que Aristote entreprist Alixandre son desciple, et Alixandre si le dist a s'amie Alchïadis si qu'elle se pensa de decevoir Aristote. Si vint une matinee pres de une tour ou Aristote estudoit, et estoit cele tour assize en une belle praerie. Si vint cele Alchïadis au pié de la tour et commensa a chanter a haute voys moult serie et belle et clere, come cele qui chantoit

plus cler et mervis que nulle autre feme; et quant Aristote l'oÿ chanter, si
se assit a la fenestre et la regarda amont et aval et ne vit nulluy que celle
feme qui si bien chantoit, et s'en si fu ainsi enflambé de l'amor de cele
feme, si descendi de la tor et la reqist cele se fi la dangerose, et en la fin li
promist et li assena terme a lendemain. Et Aristote la layssa atant et fu
moult lyés dou terme qu'elle li avoit assené. Lors elle se parti et vint a son
ami Alixandre, et li reconta tout ce qu'elle avoit fait.

Lendemain se leva cele Alcïadis et vint a la tour et porta ovec elle .i.
frayn et une selle, et fist Alexandre mucier dedens .i. arbre crois qui estoit
pres d'iluec, et elle commensa a chanter. Tantost Aristote saylli et descendi
de son estude aval la tour et commensa a parler la dite Alcïadis. Elle li
respondi que, se il voloit chevaucher sur elle, que il covenoit qu'elle le
chevauchast avant, et li meist le frayn a la bouche et la selle sur le dos.
Celuy qui estoit eschaufé l'otroya et consenti. Elle tantost l'enfrena et
l'ensella et puis li monta dessus, et il chaitif estoit a .iiii. piés auci come
une beste mue. Et lors sailly avant Alixandre et escria et reprist son maistre
Aristote et se il fu vergoingnos, nous ne le doit demander. Et revint lors
meïsmes en sa rayson come home vertuos qu'il estoit, et dist ceste parole
que touche la philosophie en ceste part, s'il a dist moult vertuosement.
"Certes," dist il, "se je eüsse eü les ziaus de lins, je n'eüsse pas esté surpris
ne enflambé de s'amor, car je eüsse vue l'ordure que est dedens son cors."

**10. Anonymous Benedictine on the Inconstant Scholar. Print [Geneva:
Jean Croquet, before 1481], unnumbered pages 46–48.**

Dont nous lisons en une histoire
Que Boëce dist qui fut voire,
Et n'est pas en cest texte mise,
Mais il mesmes si la devise
5 En ung aultre lieu qui est fait,
Dont le fist et briefment l'extrait
Celluy qui cest texte interprete,
Et en ce lieu cy le repete.
Dont cy en françois je l'expose
10 En moy conformant a la glose;
Mais ung pou plus dilaté l'ay
Pour mieulx dilater l'engin lay.
Le livre ou Boëce le dist

     Et dont ce translateur le prist
15   Est nommés de la discipline
     Des escoliers de leur doctrine.
        Et dist Boëce en celle somme
     Que jadis fut ung bon preudomme
     Qui ot ung filz moult varïable,
20   Le quel il nomma non estable,
     Qui au premier an de sa vie
     Regarda l'estat de clergie
     Et vit qu'il est trop precieux
     Tres aisie et delicieux.
25   Les clers ont les prelations,
     Les terres, les possessions,
     Les grans palefrois et chevaulx,
     Les vins vieux et les nouveaulx,
     Devant tous aultres la parole.
30   Si se print aler a l'escole
     Et cuida bon clerc devenir,
     Et ses grans estas maintenir.
     Quant aprés vint trois ans ou quatre,
     Il regarda les enfans batre
35   Et la peine qu'il convient traire
     Quant ungs homs se veult bon clerc faire.
     Matin lever et tart couchier
     De jour penser et nuyt songier
     Et des aultres afflictions
40   Qui sont vers es prelations.
     Estat de clergie desprise
     Et dist que mieulx vault marchandise.
        Marchans gaingnent hardiement.
     Marchans vivent aisiement.
45   Marchans poënt prouffit acquerre,
     Et par la mer et par la terre.   [p. 47]
     Lors fist ces nefs apparreillier,
     Oultre mer s'en va pour gaignier.
     Mais quant fut en la mer profonde
50   Regarda le peril de l'onde,
     Et lors ot le cueur moult amer

Pour le movement de la mer,
Et se prist a vomir moult fort,
Adonc plein de grant desconfort.
55   Tantost arriere s'en retourne
Pour cultiver terre s'atourne.
Et cil qui avoit cueur volage
Print trop a louer curtilege,
Car on peut gaigner en courtil
60 Sans grant traveil et grant peril,
Sans aler loing de sa maison.
Mais aprés vint une sayson
Quant il cuida grant gaing acquerre:
Sa semence pourrist en terre
65 Et ne getta germe ne grain,
Dont se tint pour ung fol villain.
      Et jura lors par sa main destre
Que chevalier le convient estre,
Car chevaliers ont les honneurs
70 Et les estas de grans seigneurs
Sans mains mettre on leur apporte;
Tout ce que leur fault a leur porte
On les sert a grant diligence
En honneur et en reverence.
75 Chascun doubte le chevalier,
Car il mene son escuier
Et ses hommes et sa pietaille;
N'est chose au monde qui le vaille.
Et s'aucun leur fait villennie
80 Il n'est pas bien seur de sa vie.
Tantost chevalier se fist faire,
Mais aprés luy vint a contraire,
Car aler le convint en guerre
Pour son pays et pour sa terre.
85 Quant s'arma selon la coustume
Des armes qui ne sont pas plume
Et puis mist le heaulme en sa teste,
Ne le tint pas a geu ne a feste.
Aprés quant vit la chevauchie

90   Des ennemis tant aprouchie
     Et qu'il ne souzetraire apart,
     Lors volsist bien estre aultrepart;
     Et pense s'il estoit delivres
     Qui luy donroit cent mille livres.
95   Cest estat il ne maintendroit
     Pour le grant peril qu'il y voit.
          Puis s'entourna aux advocas
     Et vit qu'entre tous les estas
     Est cil selon ce qui luy semble
100 Ou l'en met plus d'argent ensemble.
     Advocas gaingnent sans grant peyne
     Quant ungs homs sa cause demaine;
     Par advocas qui tousjours tire
     Il se peult bien tenir de rire,
105 Car s'il a point d'argent en bourse
     Ly advocas si luy desbourse.
     Tantost print habit d'avocat,
     De chevalier laisse l'estat.
     Quant vint aprés en ung fort plait
110 Ses adversaires avant trait
     Tant de coustumes et de drois,
     Tant de canons et tant de loys,
     Et tant de demandes luy baille.
     Qu'il ne scet de quel part il aille.
115   Si propose en son corage   [p. 48]
     Qu'il se mettra en marïage,
     Car quant on ha sa preudefame,
     Sage, subtile, de bonne fame,
     Elle gouverne sa maison
120 Et tout ordonne par rayson.
     Moult d'aises fait a son mary.
     S'elle luy voit le cueur marry
     Tresdoulcement le resconforte
     Assés d'aultre prouffis luy porte.
125 Pour ce tantost se maria
     Pour le grant desir qu'il y a.
     Aprés quant cel estat cognoit

Ne trouva pas ce qu'il cuidoit:
Or patenostres or pellissons
130 Or coyffes, queuvrechiefz, boutons,
Or robes, ciantures, anneaulx,
Or escrins et aultres joyaulx,
Or visiter pelerinages,
Or acompaignier marïages,
135 Or ses parens et ses commeres,
Or nopces et aultres miseres
Ou naturelment est enclin
Tout le sexte dit femenin.
     Dont tint en despit marïage,
140 Et se mist en ung renclusage,
Et proposa toute sa vie
Estudier astonomie
Et sçavoir du ciel la nature,
Car de la terre n'a plus cure.
145 Si commence a estudier,
De nuyt et de jour travailler.
Tant y trouva d'empeschement
De regles au commencement,
Tant de livres, tant de quadrans,
150 D'astralabes entresequens,
De chemins et retrogrades,
De cours tradeaux, de speres tardes,
Tant d'estoilles et de planetes,
De termes, de cercles, et de metes
155 Polartique et puis auctentique,
De divisions et figures
De proporcions et mesures,
De poincts, de revolucions
Et de pronosticacions
160 Des choses qui sont a avenir.
Qui ne scet qu'il doit devenir
Ains est esbahys de sa vie,
Et dist en sa melencolie
Qu'il vouldroit bien ung asne estre.
165 Ung asne ha teste champestre,

De riens du monde ne luy chault
Autant du froit comme de chault.
Cy fine l'ystoire atant.

Selected variants. MS Royal 20 A 19 has, after line 128 Si lui semble que pou s'amende / Car se femme si luy demande; *MS B. N. fr. 12459 has, after line 136* Et aprés aler aux estuves / Estuver et baignier en cuves; *MS B. N. fr. 24308 has the preferred reading for line 155 and its missing rime* Pole artique, antartique / Estoille estant et erratique; *and for the last four lines gives instead:*

Asnes ne met riens en sa teste,
De riens au monde ne li chaut
Autant du froit come du chaut;
Pour ce le dy tant seullement,
Quar en tous les estas briefment
A une malle circonstance
Qui fait desirer la muance.

For other variants of lines 1–22 and 145–end, see the article by Astrik Gabriel cited in the discussion.

11. Renaut de Louhans's stanzas on Death. MS B. N. fr. 578, fols. 27v–28.

La mort guerroye humain linage
Puis lors qu'Adam par son oultrage
La pomme deffendue mort.
Pour ce n'espargne fol ne sage
5 Homme bas ne de hault parage;
Tout couvient passer par la mort.

La mort fiert a destre et a senestre,
N'espargne lay ne clerc ne prestre
Quant afilé son fil retort.
10 Toute choses que Dieu fait nestre,
Il les couvient aprés non estre
Par la puissance de la mort.

La mort voit cardinaulx et papes,
A chascun dit, "Se tu m'eschapes,
15 Tu seras moult preuz et moult fort!"
Ja ne vous y vauldront grappes,
Or ne argent prins en voz trapes,
Atrapez serez par la mort.

     La mort prelaz aisé tenuz,
20 Fourrez de gris et vers menuz,
     Regarde et menace fort.
     Elas, com seront mal venuz!
     Ilz demourront pouvres et nuz
     Quant ilz passeront par la mort.

25   La mort vaint chanoines clergiez
     Qui sont cointement herbergiez,
     D'aisé vivre font leur effort;
     En delices sont tous plungiez.
     De vins nouveaulx et de vins viez
30 Le darrenier morsel est la mort.

     La mort assault moinnes cloistriers,
     Prescheurs, carmelins, cordeliers
     Et tous autres de leur accort.
     Ne leur y vault lire psaultiers.
35 Franchises, cloistres, ne monstiers
     Tout franchement les prent la mort.

     La mort prent les nonnains velees
     Qui seulement sont ordonnees
     Pour avoir en Dieu leur confort,
40 De blans cueuvrechiefs sont parees
     De peliçons chaux sont fourrees;
     De tout ce ne chaut a la mort.

     La mort les empereres donte,
     Roy ne doubte, ne duc, ne conte,
45 Leur rierecry ne leur effort;
     De leur hautesse ne fait compte,
     Car leur hautesse riens ne monte
     Ne leur povoir contre la mort.

     La mort fait gitter maintes lermes
50 Quant elle fiert chevaliers d'armes

Senz courtoisie et senz deport;
Ja pour paour de leurs jusarmes
Ne leur esloingnera leurs termes.
La darriers termes est la mort.

55   La mort vaint jeunes damoisiaux
Quant ilz mainnent leurs grant ainaux
Et leur deduit et leur deport.
Sur leurs poins portent les oisiaux,
Jouer s'en vont par ces bois haulx;
60 Tousjours aprés eulx court la mort.

La mort prent jeunes damoiselles
A lignies cointes et belles,
De grans atours et de hault port.
Helas, helas que feront elles?   [fol. 28]
65 Leurs testes ne seront pas telles
Quant auront sentie la mort.

La mort sur le riche villain
Qui bien ne puet yssir de main
Son serne gitte et son sort.
70 Ne lui laira ne vin ne pain
Or ne argent, robe ne grain;
Tout nu l'enportera la mort.

La mort fait tresgrant villenie
Quant a femme d'anfans chargie;
75 Son mari de ses mains estort.
La mere plaint et plore et crie,
Quant voit la petite maignie.
L'oreille sorde fait la mort.

La mort ne prise advocas
80 Ne commandement d'ypocras,
N'ont povoir qu'il li facent tort.
Ne leur y vault crier, "Cras, cras!"
Leurs emphorismes, ne leurs cas
Ja ne feront changier la mort.

85   La mort aucuns comme mauvaise
        Un po de temps tient paix et aise,
        Et puis aprés quant vient au fort;
        Elle les estraint et les baise
        Si tresfort que par la mesaise
90   Il font le sanglot de la mort.

        La mort aucuns par felonnie
        Fait long temps mener dure vie
        Et les met en grant desconfort.
        Il vivent en melencolie
95   En deffaut et en maladie
        Et puis aprés les prent la mort.

        La mort en champs, en bois, en prez
        En tous lieux est a chacun pres.
        Quant on veille et quant on dort
100   Soit deshaitiez, soit attremprés
        Tousjours va devant ou aprés;
        Et tousjours les gaite la mort.

        La mort a toutes gens a guerre,
        Pour ce court par mer et par terre,
105   Par tous arriver a son port.
        Celui que prent si fort enserre
        Qu'on ne scet ou l'on laisse querre,
        N'en quel lieu le maine la mort.

        La mort comme norrice amere
110   Souvent ou ventre de la mere
        L'enfant debroye et detort.
        Helas, pour quel cause compere
        Le pechié de son premier pere
        Le petit filz souffrant la mort.

115   La mort fu moult baude et hardie
        Quant Jhesu print, le filz Marie,

Qui nasqui d'elle senz nul tort.
Pour ce tres doulcement li prie
Qu'il nous soit aidans a la vie,
120   Et secours nous face a la mort.

Appendix II

List of All Manuscripts of the *Consolatio* in Medieval French

1. Prose version by an anonymous Burgundian (early 13th century): Wien, Österreichische Nationalbibliothek, MS 2642.
2. Prose version by an anonymous Wallonian (late 13th century): Troyes, MS 898.
3. Prose version by Bonaventura da Demena (late 13th century?): Paris, Bibliothèque Nationale, MS fr. 821.
4. Prose version by Pierre de Paris (ca. 1305–9): Città del Vaticano, Biblioteca Apostolica, MS lat. 4788.
5. Prose version by Jean de Meun (ca. 1300): Besançon, MS 434; Chantilly, Musée Condé, MSS 283, 284; Dijon, MS 525 (compilation); Douai, MS 765; New York, Pierpont Morgan Lib., MS 332; Oxford, Bodleian Lib., MS Rawlinson G 41; Paris, Bibl. de l'Arsenal, MSS 732, 733, 738, 2669 (compilation); Paris, Bibl. Nationale, MSS fr. 809 (compilation), 1097, 1098, lat. 8654B, 18424; Rennes, MS 593; Saint-Omer, MS 661.
6. Mixed prose and verse version (early 14th century): Amiens, MS 412 (incomplete); Bern, Bürgerbibl., MS 365; Montpellier, MS Med. 43; Paris, Bibl. Nationale, MS fr. 1096.
7. Revised mixed version (mid-14th century): Aberystwyth, National Library of Wales, MSS 5031, 5039; Auckland, N. Z., Public Lib., MS Sir G. Gray 119; Baltimore, Walters Gallery, MS 503; Bergues, MS 27; Bruxelles, Bibliothèque Royale, MSS 10180–93, 10222–23; Carpentras, MS 405; London, British Museum, MSS Addit. 10341, 21602, Harley 4330, 4335–9; Modena, Biblioteca Estense, MS Coll. Campori G 3 14; Montpellier, MS Med. 368; New York, Pierpont Morgan Lib., MSS 222, 396 (incomplete); New York, Pub. Lib., MS 17; Orléans, MS 415; Oxford, Bodleian Lib., MS Douce 352; Paris, Bibl. de l'Arsenal, MS 737; Paris, Bibl. Mazarine, MS 3861; Paris, Bibl. Nationale, MS J. de Rothschild 2753, MSS fr. 575, 1092, 1093, 1099, 1100–1,

1541, 1652, 1728, 1947 (incomplete), 1948, 1949, 12238 pt. 2 (incomplete), 17080, 17272, 24231, 25417, lat. 6643, nouv. acq. fr. 6535, 20001, nouv. acq. lat. 2381 (fragment); Reims, MS 879; Roanne, MS 64; Rouen, MS 3045; Sydney, MS Nicholson 7; Vaticano, Bibl. Apost., MSS Reg. lat. 1492, 1508; Wien, Öst. Natbibl., MSS 2595, 2653.

8. Verse version by the Anonymous of Meun (mid-14th century): Paris, Bibliothèque Nationale, MSS fr. 576, 1543 (incomplete).

9. Verse version by Renaut de Louhans (ca. 1336–7): Abbotsford, Scott's Library, MS I i; Arras, MS 972; Besançon, MS 422 (defective); Bruxelles, Bibl. Royale, MSS 10220, 10221, 10300, 18064; Carpentras, MS 411; Fribourg, Bibl. Cantonale et Univ., MSS 7, 161; Genève, Bibl. Publique et Univ., MSS 174d, 179bis (extracts); London, British Museum, MSS Egerton 2633, Royal 19 A IV; Mâcon, MS 95; Magdeburg, Dom–Gymnasium, MS 224 (present loc. unknown); München, Bayrische Staatsbibl., MS Gall. 31; New Haven, Yale Lib., MS 38; Paris, Bibliothèque Nationale, MSS fr. 578, 822, 1095, 1102, 1540, 1542, 1651, 19137 (defective), 24230, 24307, 24308; Toulouse, MS 817; Vaticano, Bibl. Apost., MS Reg. lat. 1518.

10. Verse revision of Renaut by an anonymous Benedictine monk (ca. 1380): Amiens, MS 411; Arras, MS 845; Bruxelles, Bibl. Royale, MS 10474; Cambridge, Trinity Hall Lib., MS 12; Chantilly, Musée Condé, MSS 285, 485; Douai, MS 766; London, British Museum, MSS Addit. 26767, Royal 20 A XIX; Orléans, MS 416; Oxford, Bodleian Lib., MSS Douce 298, Rawlinson Poet. 161; Paris, Bibl. de l'Arsenal, MS 2670; Paris, Institut de France, MS 264; Paris. Bibl. Nationale, MSS fr. 577, 812, 813 (misbound), 1094, 1946, 12237, 12238 pt. 1, 12239 (misbound), 12240, 12459 (compilation), 24309, 25416, nouv. acq. fr. 1982, 5094 (fragment); Paris, Bibl. Sainte Geneviève, MS 1132; Toulouse, MS 822; York, Min. Lib. XVI.D.14.

11. Verse abbreviation of Renaut (14th century): Paris, Bibl. Nationale, MS fr. 25418.

12. Second mixed version (early 15th century?): Aberystwyth, National Library of Wales, MS 5038.

13. Mixed version printed by Colard Mansion: Bruges, 1477 and reprinted by Antoine Verard: Paris, 1494.

The following are unassigned MSS: London, H. Y. Thompson Collection 45 and 87; Heidelberg, Univ. Lib. 484; and Berlin, Deutsche Staatsbibl., Hamilton Coll. 96 and 97.

R. H. Lucas, in "Medieval French Translations of the Latin Classics to 1500," *Speculum* 45 (1970), 225–53, adds the following possibilities which I have not been able to confirm: Possibly Version 7: Jena, Universitätsbibl. NB 87; Leningrad, Publichnaja Bibl., poet. 9Z; Turin, 1670. Possibly Version 9: Glasgow, Hunterian Museum 439; Bern, Bürgerbibl. A95 (10). Possibly Version 10: Bruxelles, Bib. Roy. 11244; Vatican, Reg. 1689.

Selected Bibliography

Benson, Larry D. "The Literary Character of Anglo–Saxon Formulaic Poetry." *PMLA* 81 (1966):334–41.

Bertoni, M. G. "Des estats du siècle." *Zeitschrift für romanische Philologie* 34 (1910):368–9.

______. *Notice sur deux manuscrits d'une traduction française de la "Consolation" de Boèce conservées à la Bibliothèque cantonale de Fribourg.* Fribourg, 1910.

Bode, Georg H., ed. *Scriptores rerum mythicarum latini tres Romae nuper reperti.* Cellis, 1834.

Boëcis: poeme sur Boèce. Edited and translated by René Lavaud and Georges Machicot. Toulouse: Institut d'Études Occitanes, 1950.

Boethius: the Theological Tractates, the Consolation of Philosophy. Edited and translated by H. F. Stewart and E. K. Rand. Loeb Classical Library. Cambridge, Mass.: Harvard Univ. Press, 1918.

Chenu, M. D. "Involucrum: le mythe selon les théologiens médiévaux." *Archives d'histoire doctrinale et littéraire du moyen âge* 22 (1955):75–9.

Cline, James M. "Chaucer and Jean de Meung." *ELH* 3 (1936):170–81.

Courcelle, Pierre. *La Consolation de philosophie dans la tradition littéraire: antécédents et postérité de Boèce.* Paris: Études Augustiniennes, 1967.

______. "Étude critique sur les commentaires de la Consolation de Boèce (IXe–XVe siècles)." *Archives d'histoire doctrinale et littéraire du moyen âge* 14 (1939):5–140.

Crespo, Roberto. "Jean de Meun traduttore della *Consolatio philosophia* di Boezio." *Atti dell' Accad. delle Scienze di Torino* 103 (1969): 65–170.

Cropp, Glynnis M. "La traduction française de la *Consolatio Philosophie* de Boèce: Encore un manuscrit." *Romania* 90 (1969):258–70.

Dedeck–Héry, V. L. "Boethius' *De Consolatione* by Jean de Meun." *Mediaeval Studies* 14 (1952):165–275.

______. "Un Fragment inédit de la traduction de la *Consolation* de Boèce par Jean de Meun." *Romanic Review* 27 (1936):110–24.

______. "Jean de Meun et Chaucer: traducteurs de la Consolation de Boèce." *PMLA* 42 (1937):967–91.

______. "The Manuscripts of the Translation of Boethius's *Consolatio* by Jean de Meung." *Speculum* 15 (1940):432–43.

Delisle, Leopold. "Anciennes traductions françaises de la consolation de Boèce conservées à la Bibliothèque Nationale." *Bibliothèque de l'École des Chartes* 34 (1873):5–32.

Denomy, A. J. "The Vocabulary of Jean de Meun's Translation of Boethius' *De Consolatione Philosophiae.*" *Mediaeval Studies* 16 (1954):19–34.

Donaghey, B. S. "Another English Manuscript of an Old French Translation of Boethius." *Medium Aevum* 42 (1973):38–42.

Dwyer, Richard A. "Another Boece." *Romance Philology* 19 (1965): 268–70.

______. "The Appreciation of Handmade Literature." *The Chaucer Review* 8 (1974):221–40.

______. "Bonaventura da Demena, Sicilian Translator of Boethius." *French Studies* 28 (1974):129–33.

______. " 'Je meurs de soif auprès de la fontaine.' " *French Studies* 23 (1969):225–8.

______. "Manuscripts of the Medieval French Boethius." *Notes & Queries* (1971):124–5.

______. "The Old French Boethius: Addendum." *Medium Aevum* 43 (1974):265–6.

______. "Old French Translations of Boethius' *Consolatio Philosophiae* in the National Library of Wales." *Nat. Lib. of Wales Journal* 14 (1966):486–8.

______. "Villon's Boethius." *Annuale Mediaevale* 11 (1970):74–80.

Fäh, Laurenz. *Die Sprache der altfranzösischen Boëthius–Übersetzung enthalten in dem Ms. 365 der Stadtbibliothek Bern.* Freiburg, 1915.

Friedman, John B. *Orpheus in the Middle Ages.* Cambridge, Mass.: Harvard Univ. Press, 1971.

Gabriel, Astrik L. "The Source of the Anecdote of the Inconstant Scholar." *Classica et Medievalia* 19 (1958):152–76.

Grigsby, John L. *The Middle French "Liber Fortunae": a Critical Edition.* University of California Publications in Modern Philology, vol. 81. Berkeley: Univ. of Calif. Press, 1967.

Gros Louis, Kenneth R. R. "Robert Henryson's *Orpheus and Eurydice* and the Orpheus Traditions of the Middle Ages." *Speculum* 41 (1966): 643–55.

Hatinguais, Jacqueline. "En marge d'un poème de Boèce: l'interpretation allegorisée du mythe d'Orphée par Guillaume de Conches." In *Actes du Congrès,* Association Guillaume Budé, Congrès de Tours et Poitiers, pp. 285–9. Paris, 1954.

Heitmann, Klaus. "Boethius' Verdammung der Musen im Mittelalter." In *Renatae Litterae.* Ed. K. Heitmann and Eckhart Schroeder, pp. 23–49. Frankfurt: Athenaeum, 1973.

Howard, Donald. *The Three Temptations: Medieval Man in Search of the World.* Princeton: Princeton Univ. Press, 1966.

Jeauneau, Édouard. "L'usage de la notion d'*integumentum* à travers les glosses de Guillaume de Conches." *Archives d'histoire doctrinale et littéraire du moyen âge* 24 (1957):35–70.

Jordan, Robert M. *Chaucer and the Shape of Creation: the Aesthetic Possibilities of Inorganic Structure.* Cambridge, Mass.: Harvard Univ. Press, 1967.

Jourdain, Charles. "Des commentaires inédits de Guillaume de Conches et Nicolas Traveth sur la Consolation de Boèce." *Notices et extraits de manuscrits de la Bibliothèque Impériale* 20, 2 (1862):40–82.

Kahrl, Stanley. "Allegory in Practice: a Study of Narrative Styles in Medieval Exempla." *Modern Philology* 63 (1965):105–10.

Kottler, Barnet. "The Vulgate Tradition of the *Consolatio Philosophiae* in the Fourteenth Century." *Mediaeval Studies* 17 (1955):209–14.

Langlois, Charles Victor. "La Consolation de Boèce d'après Jean de Meun et plusieurs autres." In *La Vie en France au moyen âge,* vol. 4, pp. 269–326. Paris, 1928.

Langlois, Ernest. "La Traduction de Boèce par Jean de Meun." *Romania* 42 (1913):331–69.

Lowes, John L. "Chaucer's Boethius and Jean de Meun." *Romanic Review* 8 (1917):383–400.

Lucas, R. H. "Medieval French Translations of the Latin Classics to 1500." *Speculum* 45 (1970):225–53.

Meyer, Paul. "Notice du ms. 10295–304 de la Bibliothèque Royale de Belgique (Légende en prose et en vers)." *Romania* 30 (1901):314.

Moll, W. "Bisschop Adelbolds commentar op een metrum van Boethius." *Kerkhistorisch Archief* 3 (1862):198–213.

Nagel, F. "Die altfranzösische Übersetzung der *Consolatio philosophiae* des Boethius von Renaut von Louhans." *Zeitschrift für romanische Philologie* 15 (1891):1–23.

Paris, Paulin. *Les Manuscrits françois de la Bibliothèque du Roi.* Vols. 5 and 6. Paris, 1842 and 1845.

Patch, Howard R. *The Goddess Fortuna in Medieval Literature.* Cambridge, Mass., 1927.

––––––. *The Tradition of Boethius: a Study of his Importance in Medieval Culture.* New York, 1935.

Payne, F. Anne. *King Alfred and Boethius.* Madison: Univ. of Wisconsin Press, 1969.

Peterson, K. O. "Chaucer and Trivet." *PMLA* 18 (1903):174–93.

[Renaut de Louhans.] "Des estats du siecle." In *Recueil général et complet des fabliaux des XIIIe et XIVe siècles,* ed. A. de Montaiglon and G. Renaud, vol. 2, pp. 264–8. Paris, 1877.

Ritter, Eugene. "Notice du ms. 179bis de la Bibliothèque de Genève." *Bulletin de la Société des anciens textes français* 3 (1877):84–113.

Silk, E. T. *Saeculi noni auctoris in Boetii consolationem philosophiae commentarius.* Papers and Monographs of the American Academy in Rome, vol. 9. Rome, 1935.

Simund de Freine. *Les Oeuvres*. Edited by John E. Matzke. Société des anciens textes français. Paris, 1909.

Sinclair, K. V. "Un Manuscrit méconnu du Boèce." *Scriptorium* 17 (1963):130–2.

Smalley, Beryl. *English Friars and Antiquity in the Early Fourteenth Century*. Oxford: Basil Blackwell, 1960.

Stewart, H. F. *Boethius: an Essay*. Edinburgh, 1891.

––––––. "A Commentary by Remigius Autissiodorensis on the *De Consolatione Philosophiae* of Boethius." *Journal of Theological Studies* 17 (1915):22–42.

Stone, Louise. "Old French Translations of the *De Consolatione Philosophiae* of Boethius: Some Unnoticed MSS." *Medium Aevum* 6 (1937): 21–30.

Thomas, Antoine. "Jean de Sy et Jean de Cis." *Romania* 21 (1892): 612–5.

––––––. "Notice sur le manuscrit latin 4788 du Vatican." *Notices et extraits des manuscrits de la Bibliothèque Nationale* 41 (1917):29–90.

––––––. and Mario Roques. "Traductions françaises de la *Consolatio Philosophiae* de Boèce." In *Histoire littéraire de la France,* vol. 37, pp. 419–88. Paris, 1938.

Van de Vyver, A. "Les Traductions du *De Consolatione Philosophiae* de Boèce en littérature comparée." *Humanisme et Renaissance* 6 (1939): 247–73.

Van Hasselt, André. *Essai sur l'histoire de la poésie en Belgique*. Memoires couronnés par l'Academie de Bruxelles, vol. 13. Bruxelles, 1838.

Wenzel, Siegfried. *The Sin of Sloth: "Acedia" in Medieval Thought and Literature*. Chapel Hill: Univ. of North Carolina Press, 1967.

Index of Names